For Henry Rosovsky:
with admiration
and ap... —A
your ...
K-12 eff...s.
Best regards,
Ben Tregoe
March 11, 1998

THE CULTURE
OF SUCCESS

THE CULTURE OF SUCCESS

Building a Sustained Competitive Advantage
by Living Your Corporate Beliefs

John Zimmerman, Sr.

With Benjamin B. Tregoe

McGraw-Hill

New York   San Francisco   Washington, D.C.   Auckland   Bogotá
Caracas   Lisbon   London   Madrid   Mexico City   Milan
Montreal   New Delhi   San Juan   Singapore
Sydney   Tokyo   Toronto

McGraw-Hill

A Division of The **McGraw·Hill** Companies

1 2 3 4 5 6 7 8 9 0   DOC/DOC   9 0 2 1 0 9 8 7

ISBN 0-07-073008-3

The sponsoring editor for this book was Susan Barry, the editing supervisor was Fred Dahl, and the production supervisor was Pamela Pelton. It was set in Fairfield by Inkwell Publishing Services.

Printed and bound by R. R. Donnelley and Sons Company.

McGraw-Hill books are available at special quantity discounts to use as premiums and sales promotions, or for use in corporate training programs. For more information, please write to the Director of Special Sales, McGraw-Hill, 11 West 19th Street, New York, NY 10011. Or contact your local bookstore.

CONTENTS

ACKNOWLEDGMENTS

A most grateful thanks to the executives of the four companies who opened their doors to our research and exploration of their basic beliefs, how they were working, and how the process might be improved. Those results are a key part of this book. Thanks also to the 771 employees in those companies who responded to our written basic beliefs survey. All of the executives who participated in the interviews are identified in Chap. 8 through 11. A special thanks to Wayne Campton, Director of Quality and Education, The American Automobile Association; Paul Kerins, Chief Human Resources Executive, Barnett Banks, Inc.; Bill Gray, Vice President of Human Resources, Harley-Davidson, Inc.; and Bob Ellis, Vice President of Human Resources, The J. M. Smucker Company. They coordinated all of our research with their companies.

William A. Schiemann and his staff at the Metrus Group in Somerville, New Jersey reviewed and made major improvements to the basic beliefs survey we used with the four companies participating in the book.

My deepest appreciation to my colleague, Ben Tregoe, for thirty-six years of leadership, inspiration, and friendship. He stimulated my interest in this subject. Thanks also, Ben, for your support and participation in this project.

This book was much improved from the thoughtful and penetrating critique of my business colleagues and friends Bob Morison, Stan Sawczuk, and Ben Tregoe; the executives of the four participating companies; and my four sons, John Jr., Paul, Mark, and Jim. My sons felt it might be a bit difficult to critique their father. Let me tell you that they did and I knew they would. Thank you all.

Thanks to son Mark for creating the computer program for data selection and generating the output from the written surveys and to Marie Zimmerman for data entry and Jim Vandegriff for classifying the essay question responses.

To Debbie Zimmerman, who painstakingly and always pleasantly typed the seven revisions leading to the final version, I give unending and fond thanks for her efforts and her patience with me.

Finally to my wife, Charlotte, I say with much love, "You made it work." She helped me organize and then typed the detailed survey result reports for the four companies. She worked with each draft of the book to make me take my long and sometimes cumbersome sentences apart and rework them for the reader. She organized all the footnotes and kept track of all the critiques to see that I took full advantage of the feedback. She graciously accepted my moods and pressures over the two years of this project.

John Zimmerman, Sr.

INTRODUCTION

Ben Tregoe and I have always believed in the importance of basic beliefs. Ours guided us and kept us on track as Kepner-Tregoe, Inc. ("K-T") grew from its beginnings in a California garage in 1958 to a worldwide consulting organization. Our business was helping organizations improve their day-to-day operational problem solving and decision making. It was interesting that those companies that had serious operational troubles were not the ones we worked with. Most often our clients were doing a reasonably good job at problem solving and decision making, but they saw we had some ideas that might make them even better. Years later we encountered the same phenomenon in companies whose senior management we worked with in improving strategic decision making. From this experience, across many levels in a corporation, we saw an increasing importance placed on basic beliefs as key drivers of strategic and operational decision making. We became convinced that good corporations with longer-term perspectives had a basic beliefs process and were exerting an effort to make it work.

But we also saw that a lot could be done to improve the impact of basic beliefs on long-range corporate stability and growth. Down on the factory floor at the problem-solving level, we often saw more emphasis on "Who did this?" and shifting the problem to someone else rather than looking for the cause and solving the problem. We saw short-term pressures produce costly interim fixes rather than long-term solutions. We heard work groups saying, "Our managers don't want us to think."

Often at the strategic level we found that it was our focus on basic beliefs that caused top management to realize the influence of beliefs on their strategic deliberations.

By the early 1990s, the importance of values and beliefs seemed to be decreasing across all segments of society: family, politics, education, and business. Japan and Germany had knocked our socks off on quality, value, and price. The savings and loan industry took risks beyond any fiduciary responsibility and went broke. The financial community and business schools put increasing emphasis on managing and caring about money rather than the product and the customer. Downsizing and restructuring didn't help those involved or the public in general to think business had many enduring beliefs.

Ben and I admired the values of those we knew in the business world from top to bottom. But we felt basic beliefs required more attention. They were critical in making sure that necessary short-term decisions didn't compromise long-term reputation, stability, and growth. We considered them an organization's primary long-term competitive advantage. We saw successful companies reaching those same conclusions. We thought about putting our views, research, and experience down on paper: a book to help anyone in an organization who wants to improve the influence of basic beliefs on sustained success.

We also felt there were organizations that saw the potential of beliefs, but were confused by the naysayers who said there were no proven connections between the application of beliefs and corporate success. We just plain didn't agree. We wanted to convince organizations there were ways to improve the impact of beliefs on long-term success no matter where they were in the process—from initial recognition that beliefs might be of help to extensive experience and full buy-in.

We decided to do some in-depth survey work with a few companies that had realized the importance of beliefs and were working hard to apply them. The companies we chose were The American Automobile Association, Harley-Davidson, Inc., Barnett Banks, Inc., and The J. M. Smucker Company.

In our previous work together in K-T and on other books we have written, Ben and I worked in total partnership, including knock-down critiques and debate concerning differences of opinion until we reached agreement. That was great fun and often led to one plus one equals three. But as research on this project proceeded, Ben's continuing commitment to K-T and his new personal, non-profit venture to bring problem-solving thinking into the public education system were requiring the majority of his immense creativity and time. As a result, he was relieved to take a supporting role and I was excited to proceed with the project.

As the survey work progressed and extensive library research was carried out, the importance of basic beliefs to sustain long-range corporate stability and growth was documented. We found companies making a significant effort toward applying them in the corporate world, and yet gaps in applying their full power to strategic and operational decision making surfaced. There was also the public's perception that the business world lacked beliefs: The business press and the media in general tended to make more out of the negatives than the positives.

It is my hope that as more companies focus on their basic beliefs and improve the process of putting them to work, two things will happen. First, the incidence of beliefs malpractice—or acting counter to stated beliefs—will be reduced. Second, the positive impact of basic beliefs on corporate results and on all employees, customers, and investors will be fully demonstrated.

This book is written to provide ideas and approaches to all those who want to make their basic beliefs process more effective. Whether you are an executive, a manager, a professional, a team leader, or a worker on the line, I hope this book will energize you to make your company's beliefs an even more important part of your decision making, activity, and life. In addition to the tangible benefits, it will make you sleep better at night.

One final caveat: If you are a dedicated short-term, get in–get out, take it now operator, don't bother reading this book. It will only confuse you.

THE NEED TO BELIEVE IN BELIEFS

The following is a series of what I label basic belief break-downs. They have all appeared in well-known publications. Each is briefly described under the headline by which it was reported. All the organizations involved have been around for a long time, are large, and are well enough known that they can be assumed to have some semblance of basic beliefs. But the beliefs seem to be in neglect or broken. The extent and diversity of the examples will show that the problem is widespread. Beyond that they are presented for two reasons: first, to demonstrate the need for sound basic beliefs; second, to help you determine if the basic beliefs structure in your company would prevent a similar situation or spot it early enough to stomp it out.

HEADLINE: ADM AGREES TO $100 MILLION FINE FOR PRICE-FIXING

> "In addition to the criminal fines, ADM agreed to pay $95 million to settle civil suits related to the investigation."[1]

HEADLINE: ARCHER DANIELS INDICTMENTS

> "The other shoe finally dropped at Archer Daniels Midland. On Dec. 3, the government handed down long-expected indictments of three of the ag products company's executives for price-fixing: Michael Andreas, the former ADM vice-chairman, now on leave; Terrance Wilson, a recently resigned group vice-present; and Mark Whitacre, former head of one of the ADM units allegedly involved in the scheme. The three face up to three years each in prison and $350,000 in fines."[2]

HEADLINE: *THE FALL OF A TIMBER BARON: WHY LOUISIANA-PACIFIC'S BOARD DECIDED TO DUMP HARRY MERLO (CEO)*

"For years, there had been troubling reports that LP's wood substitute [OSB—oriented strand board]—its most profitable product—was defective when used as exterior siding. … The company was all but certain to be indicted by a federal grand jury in Colorado for environmental violations and fraud involving its manufacturing processes…. Shares tumbling from all-time high of 44 in early 1994 to 22 last spring."[3]

HEADLINE: *SOMETHING SMELLS FOWL: THE ESPY SCANDAL IS MINOR COMPARED WITH THE WAY USDA HAS FAVORED THE POULTRY INDUSTRY*

This breakdown in the most fundamental beliefs and standards needs some details. *Time* magazine reported: "At least 60% of U.S. poultry is contaminated with salmonella, camphylobacter or other micro-organisms…. Each year at least 6.5 million and possibly as many as 80 million people get sick from chicken…. The conservative estimate is that bad chicken kills at least 1,000 people each year and costs several billion dollars annually in medical costs and lost productivity." Why?

First, "Everything changed in 1978. Based on a single study now considered flawed by independent experts, … USDA allowed the poultry industry to wash rather than to trim chickens and also to speed up the production lines…. Washing … merely removes the visible fecal matter while forcing harmful bacteria into the chicken's skin and body cavity." Second, "The slaughtering process today further increases the likelihood of cross-contamination as dirty birds mingle with clean ones…. The birds lose almost any chance of emerging clean when thousands at a time bathe in the 'chill tank' in order to lower their temperature prior to packing." Third, poor working conditions contribute to the problem. "Antoinette Poole quit … after working at a Tyson plant … for five years. Her job: scooping up chicken breasts that fell off the processing line and onto the factory floor…. Poole claims she was so overworked that chicken parts sometimes sat on the floor for as long as half an hour. 'Sometimes it stinks to high heaven,

but who cares? Once it's frozen it ain't gonna smell bad.' ...
If the chicken parts seemed bad, Poole was permitted to trim
or condemn them. But, 'I got intimidated by supervisors if I
threw too much into the condemned barrel,' Poole says. 'Supervisors get bonuses for saving as much chicken as possible.'" Fourth, "Merril Pipes, a sanitation employee ... says,
'We asked why we're required to package chicken that smells
bad, and they said the chicken can smell bad due to bacteria
but it can still be of good quality. That's bull as far as I'm concerned.'"[4]

HEADLINE: THE BIG SLEAZE IN MUNI BONDS

"Every year the US government gives up some $20 billion in
tax revenues to subsidize the $1.2 trillion municipal bond
market.... But as with many taxpayer-subsidized projects,
what all this easy money breeds is a thick layer of sleaze atop
many municipal financings." For example: Dr. Billy Collins,
husband of then Kentucky Governor Martha Layne Collins,
went to prison for regularly demanding that Wall Street firms
pay him if they wanted to do municipal bond business in the
state. Donaldson, Lufkin & Jenrette paid him $35,000 with
which he bought a grand piano for his wife.

Political contributions or gifts are paid to municipal officers
in return for underwriting business, a so-called "pay to play
deal." Recently passed government restrictions are full of
holes and Wall Streeters say privately they are laughably in-
effective. "Yieldburning is a method by which an investment
bank pads the bill for Treasury securities it buys on behalf of
a municipal client. It sounds mysterious, but at the bottom,
burning yield is no different from a dishonest butcher putting
his thumb on the scale. The taxpayer, not the shopper, end[s]
up taking the hit." No one knows the total taxpayer loss, but
one source puts it at $500 million to $1 billion from 1991 to
1993. "Says an unusually frank investment banker: 'Yieldburning? That's been going on for years. And, hey, I'm one of
the thieves.'"[5]

HEADLINE: A MEA CULPA—AND A COMEBACK?

Federal investigators probe charges that Caremark International, Inc., a Northbrook, Illinois, health care company, paid

kickbacks to physicians in return for referrals within its home infusion, oncology, hemophilia, and human-growth-hormone businesses. CEO C. A. Piccolo's battle ended June 16, 1995, when Caremark agreed to plead guilty and pay $159 million in civil damages and criminal fines. This was among the largest health care fraud settlements ever obtained. The stock dropped from $26 to $17—now at $21.[6]

HEADLINE: UNTANGLING THE DERIVATIVES MESS

"… [W]ild market swings turned many derivatives players into big losers last year. What magnified those losses and sent a troubling message to regulators was disturbing instances of managerial blindness, desperate behavior, even outright fraud…. The preeminent purveyor of leading-edge derivatives, Bankers Trust, was censured and fined by regulators for its role in Gibson's [the greeting card company] loss." Bankers Trust's then CEO, Charles Sanford, tended to believe it was "two guys guilty of rogue behavior." Says a former Bankers managing director in its derivatives business: "This is very much a management issue…. If you go for several years paying and promoting certain kinds of sales people, the message gets across that what they do is acceptable behavior."[7]

HEADLINE: THE BANKERS TRUST TAPES

"To substantiate its claim that a 'culture of greed and duplicity' was an element of the general climate in parts of Bankers derivatives business, P&G cites a videotaped training session for new employees. At the session, a bank employee tells his charges that, in a hypothetical derivative transaction among Sony, IBM, and Bankers Trust, 'what Bankers Trust can do for Sony and IBM is get in the middle and rip them off—take a little money.'" Bankers Trust says this comment was taken out of context.[8]

HEADLINE: A GREATER THREAT THAN TERRORISM? LAX STANDARDS FOR PLANE MECHANICS MAY COMPROMISE SAFETY

"It is impossible to determine from NTSB [National Transportation Safety Board] records whether improperly certified mechanics have been the cause of any airline accident. But a 1993 audit by the Transportation Dept.'s Inspector General's

Office paints a frightening picture of laxity and loopholes in the certification process ... 'FAA cannot be assured that only qualified applicants were certified as aviation mechanics.'"

The following paraphrases what the article said about this point:

THE FAA REGULATION	THE REALITY
Mechanics must read, write, and understand English.	Some licensed mechanics allegedly can't read English-language aircraft repair manuals.
Mechanics must have 30 months of relevant experience.	Lenient or uninformed FAA inspectors often approve candidates with irrelevant experience.
Mechanics must have 1,900 hours of an FAA-approved aviation school.	Some schools are diploma mills that teach how to pass tests, not mechanical skills.
Mechanics must pass a series of written tests to prove their aviation knowledge.	Test questions are available in advance, so the answers are typically memorized.
They must pass an oral and practical test.	Examiners set their own fees, which critics say encourages some to pass untrained students.

The article continues:

"Although the NTSB says several major airlines have been involved ... the problem is far more widespread at the low-cost carriers.... [T]here are roughly 125,000 licensed A&P mechanics in the U.S. today. Most, say airline sources, are dedicated, competent workers whose credentials are first-rate. The problem is that airlines and aircraft-repair facilities have no way of telling them apart from incompetent mechanics: They all carry the same stamp of approval from the FAA."[9]

HEADLINE: THE GOODWILL PILL MESS

"Eli Lilly proudly announced the largest product donation in their history to The Rwandan Refugee Crisis. The press release went on to say, 'This is yet another example of Lilly's commitment to giving, especially in times of human tragedy.'"

The gift was an antibiotic called CeclorCD which is not on the World Health Organization's list of essential drugs for refugees. Nor is it on treatment schedules of any countries in Central Africa. The leading relief group, Doctors Without Borders, says it would never prescribe such a medication in the camps. Lilly sent enough for 1,300,000 people in barrels containing 200,000 tablets each and with only a handful of inserts (in English) to explain usage. Today, aid workers are still trying to figure out how to dispose of 6 million pills. Many have passed their expiration dates. Dr. Hans Hogerzeil says 45 percent of donations received by the WHO office in Zagreb were either worthless or expired. In Sudan aid workers have received contact-lens solution and appetite stimulants—a bizarre contribution to a country experiencing famine. "While international health officials stress that a majority of gifts are genuine and deeply appreciated, they want to put a stop to donations that may be motivated in part by interests other than those of the recipients."[10]

HEADLINE: TEXACO SETTLES FOR 176.1 M

"Texaco agreed to pay $176.1 million to settle a 2-year-old race discrimination suit yesterday, 11 days after it was disclosed that top executives had been caught on tape belittling blacks and plotting to destroy documents in the case.... Texaco suspended two executives and apologized, ... Texaco acknowledged that the tone of the conversation was still troubling, and it did not dispute that the executives talked of trying to hide evidence.... 'With this litigation behind us, we can now move forward on our broader, urgent mission to make Texaco a model of workplace opportunity for all men and women,' said Peter I. Bijur, Texaco's chairman and chief executive, in a statement."[11]

While the above examples show beliefs negligence by U.S.-based companies, beliefs violations are not restricted to this country.

HEADLINE: UNDER SUSPICION: LE TOUT BUSINESS ELITE

In early 1996, three of France's most respected business leaders and CEOs—Louis Schweitzer of Renault, Andre Levy-Lang of Paribas and Martin Bouygues of Bouygues—

have been placed under investigation by French magistrates for allegations ranging from bribery to accounting fraud. A fourth former CEO, Loik Le Floch-Prigent of Elf Aquitaine, is likely to face interrogators.[12]

HEADLINE: SOMETHING'S ROTTEN IN ... GERMANY?

"This summer, Germans learned that prosecutors suspected dozens of employees at auto maker Adam Opel of extracting kickbacks from suppliers eager for building contracts. The probe has so far implicated 244 people at 40 companies and triggered the sudden resignations of three top Opel executives. No one has been charged ... but the news has forced Germans to admit publicly that corruption is no stranger to their country."[13]

HEADLINE: TWILIGHT OF THE GODS

A scandal touching Italy's Big Three signals the end of an era. The careers of former Fiat chairman, Gianni Agnelli, and current chairman, Cesare Romiti, and honorary chairman Enrico Cuccia of Mediobanca (Fiat's financial backbone) are drawing to a close. "But the passing of the baton could also be tainted with scandal. Gemina, the Milanese holding company in which Fiat and Mediobanca have long been key players, faces potential criminal charges for irregularities that could include falsified balance sheets, tax evasion, and insider trading."[14]

HEADLINE: WEB OF SHAME AT HONDA

Jim Cardiges, former American Honda senior vice president, his boss, John Billmyer, American Honda vice president of auto sales, and eleven other Honda officers were indicted. "Indictments handed down last week in Concord, New Hampshire, after a year long investigation, allege thirteen years of corruption and racketeering in Honda's U.S. sales organization, with $10 million in illegal transactions." Cardiges meticulously recorded a $45,042 kickback he allegedly received from the "sale" of a Honda franchise, a $30,000 grand piano, a $20,000 karaoke machine, cars, cash, jewelry, oriental rugs, and ownership interest from Honda dealers. "Eight of the indicted have pleaded guilty to single-count charges and could be sentenced to five- to 10-year prison terms by summer."[15]

HEADLINE: FEDS SHUT DAIWA'S OPERATIONS

"Indictment alleges cover-up by execs.... [A] cover-up of $1.1 billion in bond trading losses.... The cover-up, initially blamed by bank management on one rogue New York bond trader, actually reached up the ladder of Daiwa Bank.... Other than BCCI, international banking experts couldn't recall another instance where U.S. authorities shut down a foreign bank for supervisory reasons.... Iguchi [the supposed rogue] told a federal judge that his superiors directed him to continue covering up his losses in the two months before the bank publicly disclosed the scandal.... Masahiro Tsuda, the former manager of Daiwa's New York branch, was indicted, along with the bank."[16]

HEADLINE: THE DAIWA COVERUP WILL BACKFIRE ON THE BANKS

"MOF's [Japan's mighty Ministry of Finance] withholding of the facts enrages U.S.—and damages credibility worldwide.... The Daiwa mess is likely to raise more questions about the true state of Japan's other banks."[17]

HEADLINE: MR. COPPER

"Sumitomo trading scandal recalls the unpleasantness of Daiwa affair.... Fresh revelations of $1.8 billion in losses racked up by a Sumitomo trader.... Sumitomo stressed that the trader, Yasuo Hamanaka, was acting alone." He kept the same job since 1972, although it is customary in Japanese trading companies to rotate every couple of years. Hamanaka was big and known in copper—he traded 5% of the world market each year. "The revelations raise the question of whether others at Sumitomo knew about these enormous losses and helped cover them up as long as Hamanaka ostensibly was producing large profits."[18]

HEADLINE: DESCENT INTO THE ABYSS

"And the aftershocks may eventually reach into the company's top executive ranks. Three LME [London Metal Exchange] board members tell *Business Week* it's inconceivable Sumitomo officials did not know the extent of Hamanaka's trades. 'There is nothing Hamanaka was doing that wasn't done with the intimate knowledge of senior people at Sumitomo,' says one."[19]

HEADLINE: SUMITOMO TRADER

> "... Sumitomo Corp. said yesterday it will seek criminal charges against its former star copper trader for allegedly amassing $2.6 billion in losses ... far more than originally thought. Sumitomo's effort to press charges ... reinforces its assertion that the once high-flying trader acted alone, without the knowledge or participation of company managers. Sumitomo president Kenji Miyanara ... reiterated the company's 'regret and embarrassment over these extraordinary violations' of 'long-standing, clearly stated ethical and professional standards.'"[20]

Corporate basic beliefs are important. They should drive strategic and operational decisions that lead to long-term corporate stability, growth, profitability, and reputation. I have spent a lot of my career helping organizations around the world sharpen their appreciation and application of that idea. I love the world of business and free enterprise and all the values, dedication, creativity, perseverance, and hard work it takes to make it happen. To me, it has always been the high ground.

But more recently I have been appalled and saddened by all these widely publicized belief-based troubles organizations around the world are having. At the same time, more and more customers, investors, and employees consider the character and reputation of a company as part of their decision when buying a product or service, investing in, or working for that company.

Throughout this book many published examples are given of companies that have experienced significant problems from failure to have or apply basic beliefs. They are not cited to malign or show guilt but to draw attention to the importance of basic beliefs. As of this writing many of the problems are not fully resolved. I also present many examples that show the positive results of sound basic beliefs. They are not presented to make those organizations seem to be exemplars of good behavior, but rather to illustrate situationally and practically the power of basic beliefs. I do not attempt to set up a "good guys" versus "bad buys" contrast. The only connection I make is to the power of beliefs to reduce the negatives and increase the positives.

Ben Tregoe and I wanted to expand our knowledge first-hand of how basic beliefs are seen and used throughout an organization. Detailed written surveys were conducted in four companies. These companies were selected because they were noncompetitive, represented different industries, and had each applied significant effort to its basic beliefs process. The four companies are: The American Automobile Association, Harley-Davidson, Inc., Barnett Banks, Inc., and The J. M. Smucker Company. The surveys sampled all levels and functions and included in-depth follow-up interviews with senior executives. The conclusions from the interviews and the 771 surveys that were completed and returned form a key part of this book. A copy of the written survey is found in Appendix A.

Throughout this book the words "basic beliefs" and "basic beliefs process" will be used frequently. They are defined as follows.

Basic Beliefs. Those critical ethic and merit principles that guide the decisions and behavior of every employee to produce sustained success for the organization.

Basic Beliefs Process. How to put basic beliefs to work.

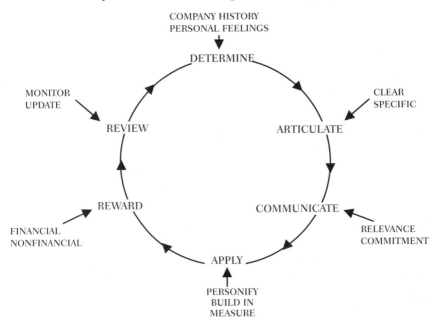

Companies and the business literature often refer to codes of ethics, ethics officers, or ethics training. This would tend to imply that ethics equals basic beliefs. This is not totally true and far too simplistic. Basic beliefs have two quite independent components.

ETHIC BELIEFS

Ethics are defined as standards of conduct and moral judgment. Ethic beliefs come from strong feelings about what kinds of moral positions and relationships make for business success. They guide performance and relationships. Ethic beliefs have a specific connotation of right or wrong. Honesty, trust, legality, and equality are examples. Ethic beliefs, then, drive decisions about how we will relate to each other and guide the work of the organization.

MERIT BELIEFS

Merit beliefs are other fundamental precepts or values that are deemed critical to an organization's success, but are neither right nor wrong in general. Merit beliefs are guiding principles that stem from deep thinking, analysis, strong feelings, and experience. Some merit beliefs have a degree of acceptance along a continuum. Level of quality, market or technological position, size, empowerment, participation, and decentralization are examples. Some merit beliefs are absolute. Maintaining independence and diversity are examples. Merit beliefs drive decisions about the kind of business a company strives to be in.

It is true that both ethic beliefs and merit beliefs guide strategic as well as operational decisions. Experience suggests that merit beliefs are more useful at the strategic level—helping to shape and define decisions about products and services, markets and customers, resource or capability requirements, and result expectations. On the other hand, ethic beliefs are more useful at the operational level—helping to shape and define policies, procedures, and practices that set the culture and behavior of the organization and determine how work is accomplished.

The following are sample basic belief statements taken from the four companies in our survey. The complete text of their basic beliefs is included later in the book.

COMPANY	MERIT BELIEF	ETHIC BELIEF
The J. M. Smucker Co.	We will remain an independent company	Highest personal ethics
Harley-Davidson, Inc.	Encourage intellectual curiosity	Tell the truth
The American Automobile Association	Only offer products that add value to membership	Equality in employment, opportunity and potential for advancement
Barnett Banks, Inc.	Nationally recognized standard in the financial services industry	Barnett people are caring and proud

Any well-thought-out short list of basic beliefs will include both ethic and merit belief inputs.

Chapters 1 and 2 explore the need for basic beliefs and their power to contribute to long-term, sustained growth and success. The next five chapters provide ideas and techniques to improve the basic beliefs process. Chapters 8 to 11 explore the ways the companies in our survey use basic beliefs to produce results. The final two chapters delve into pitfalls that can get in the way of beliefs and future challenges that need to be addressed.

EXPLORING THE NEED

The scope and variety of the examples that opened this chapter suggest there are many lessons to be learned about the need for basic beliefs and a process to make them work. The following examples provide more depth to illustrate those lessons from very different perspectives.

The first example is a top-level corporate failure to have or consider ethic beliefs, leading to dishonest short-term revenue and profit gains and skewed personal compensation. These may produce long-term consequences for customers, investors, and employees.

> Bausch & Lomb ex-CEO Daniel Gill's insistence on double-digit growth at almost any cost had led B&L executives and managers to falsify invoices and ship unwanted goods to customers. *Business Week* goes on to say: "Nowhere were the true corporate priorities clearer than in the weighting of Gill's own bonus plan: 30% depended on sales growth, 30% on earnings growth, and 30% on return on equity, another earnings-related measure. Improvement in customer satisfaction rated just 10%. At that, Gill's pay structure differs little from most ·U.S. CEOs'. He [Gill] says, 'I don't mean to pass the buck, but … as chairman I'd have only a general understanding of what happened.' Gill also professes astonishment that any B&L exec could have gotten the message that ethics should take a back seat to numerical goals. 'I have no idea' why people would believe that, he says. 'We think we are the most honorable beings on the face of the earth.'"[21]

What are the lessons? First, the Board of Directors must know the beliefs and test to see that they are built into the CEO's decision making. Second, if you are going to set high, hard goals, make sure you have a set of beliefs in place that is tied to how those goals are accomplished. Everyone down the line needs to know what ethical limits are attached to decisions made to achieve those goals. Third, establish a beliefs audit function that covers all levels. This can be done through a beliefs audit team put in place by a basic beliefs officer or committee. The team should have a rotating membership composed of executives, managers, and employees. Finally, company beliefs must guide bonus and pay schemes so there is a good balance between short- and long-term and between financial and nonfinancial performance measures.

The next example demonstrates a failure to supervise the application of beliefs, allowing a cover-up of extensive false profits by an individual.

At GE's Kidder Peabody, Joe Jett allegedly generated, or was allowed to generate, $350 million in phony trading profits. Not big for GE, but the significance of Kidder's problems reaches far beyond GE's income statement. Michael Carpenter, now resigned, came from GE Capital to run Kidder. He sought to impose GE's powerful business ethic. The first point in his six-point plan was to reestablish the firm's total commitment to integrity. For the first four years of his tenure he was not licensed to manage the broker-dealers he was charged with revitalizing. Edward Cerullo supervised Jett. After the scandal broke, Cerullo resigned amid criticism of his lack of supervision of Jett. Jett's success at trading was unprecedented, unquestioned, and unreal. He says GE made him "the fall guy." A *Fortune* article continues: "The Lynch Report [commissioned by Jack Welch] says, 'Time and again questions about Jett's unusual trading profits were answered incorrectly, ignored, or evaded.... As his profitability increased, skepticism about Jett's activities was often dismissed or unspoken.' ... For Jack Welch, one of the most widely admired Chief Executives in American business, the unfolding Kidder story is surely the stuff of bad dreams."[22]

What are the lessons? First, if your organization is in a business with fairly independent relationships between employers and customers, make sure those in charge understand and are committed to the organization's beliefs and have specific plans to implement them down through that business. Second, if the person in charge is new to the business, make sure he or she learns enough about it to know how to interpret and apply corporate beliefs. Third, when anyone in a business unit produces a short-term result far beyond any expectation, see that this performance is known about at several levels. Fourth, each of us knows when we are stepping beyond the boundaries of known beliefs, as well as the reasons why some performance is so unusual. Don't allow yourself to be "the fall guy." Finally, when actions fly in the face of beliefs such as honesty and integrity and compromise long-term for short-term gain, don't procrastinate—act. Get to the cause, correct it, and publicize the fact.

The final example shows a failure to apply well-ingrained corporate beliefs all through the organization so as to control a gradually emerging major customer problem.

The Dow Corning breast implant disaster is a most tragic example of an organization known for its beliefs and, now, the consequences of its failure to apply them. As reported instances of customer difficulties with breast implants mounted, the management of the division making them and the corporate legal staff continued to feel that Dow Corning's research and testing had been sound. According to John A. Byrne, author of *Informed Consent,* they felt it was a business issue and not one relating in any way to violations of company beliefs about quality or protecting the customer. John Swanson disagreed. Swanson monitored the company's statement of beliefs, called "The Matter of Integrity." "Swanson had created, overseen, and sustained a highly respected ethics program that had been the subject of three Harvard Business School case studies.[23] ... Swanson believed his company had failed to live up to its own code of conduct on at least two major points ... 'be responsible for the impact of Dow Corning's technology upon the environment' and 'continually strive to assure that our products and services are safe, efficacious and accurately represented in our selling and promotional activities.' Dow Corning's senior management, of course, did not believe the breast implant issue was an ethical problem. And despite his suggestions to the contrary, Swanson and the Business Conduct Committee had not been asked to get involved."[24]

At his retirement presentation Swanson laid out what he felt it took to have beliefs work. "Swanson urged the company to decentralize its efforts, making line managers accountable for conducting ethics reviews and bringing the code of business conduct to life ... the idea would be to hold many group sessions on ethics more frequently. Ethics ... had to be a periodic but regular agenda item in staff meetings throughout the organization and at every level. All these activities would be overseen by area Business Conduct Committees, each with a communications and feedback channel that would allow any employee at any time to raise concern about an ethical issue without fear of retribution."[25]

While it doesn't solve the problem entirely, there is now evidence to support Dow Corning's point of view: "In recent years, epidemiologists from institutions such as the Mayo Clinic & Foundation and Harvard University—who studied thousands of women with implants—failed to find a link between the devices and maladies such as scleroderma, joint pain, chronic fatigue, and arthritis."[26]

Although much of this issue is still in the courts, some resolution has begun: "many medical and legal experts have long suspected that the blame laid on implants is based on 'junk science.' ... [I]n a bold opinion that surprised legal experts across the country, a federal district court judge in Portland, Oregon, endorsed that view. Expert testimony linking implants to 'any systemic disorder ... of any kind,' Judge Robert E. Jones declared, was so lacking in scientific credibility that it didn't belong in the courtroom."[27]

Whatever the ultimate conclusion, much damage has been done to Dow Corning's reputation. The irony is that this product generated less than one percent of the company's revenue.

A major lesson to be learned from this example is that enforcement of beliefs cannot be vested in an ethics officer or committee. Through the basic beliefs process, responsibility for applying beliefs must rest in the person making a decision or handling a problem. No emerging customer problem, particularly one involving a possible product defect and physical health, should be addressed without looking at basic beliefs and long-term impact. Management above the level where the problem exists must see that basic beliefs are considered in any analysis and resolution.

These major examples create obvious concern. But there are also many nonsensational, day-to-day decisions with negative outcomes made because beliefs aren't applied, and these may have even greater impact. The following individual responses are quoted directly from our survey respondents when we asked:

"Please describe an important decision about which you feel the outcome was negative because the basic beliefs were not applied."

The American Automobile Association

- Resources allocated for telecommunications enhancements at an AAA Club were withheld to enable the company to secure a stronger short-term financial position. While the decision was reasonable and understandable, it did not place our members (customers) as its number one priority. Furthermore, we continue to wrestle with phone problems today.

- Establishment of a member service center at an AAA Club a few years ago ... was designed with cost containment and management control as the driving force rather than member satisfaction and value-added considerations. We are now working to change this structure and the culture.

- Negative outcome resulted when local political considerations at an AAA Club were deemed more important than basic beliefs in determining the geographic location of a significant member service facility.

Harley-Davidson, Inc.

- Forming a business alliance with (*name withheld*), a poor quality vendor ... not adequately screened as a vendor. An executive decision without listening to those in the know.

- A job posting was distributed when the position was already filled. This ... violates all our values.

- Allocation of resources to business units or projects we should not be in.

- At the end of every quarter, extra efforts are requested to make sure financial results are better than prior year. This is done for only a few stakeholders at the expense of other stakeholders.

Barnett Banks, Inc.

- Production guidelines (calls per hour, talk time) lessen the quality of service we offer in telebanking.

- A hardware decision ... was not made for economic or technical reasons but for political and personal reasons. As a result, operating costs are higher and service quality is lower.

- When telling employees that their positions are being eliminated, do not do it just two days before "employee appreciation day." I understand that business decisions are important; however, how can this make an employee feel? Certainly this does not make them feel like "Team Barnett."
- Meeting a project completion date at all costs. Sometimes project completion dates must slide to protect the integrity and quality of the project.
- Uncooperative lobby teller refused to help drive-in teller. Drive-in teller was backed up. Results were very angry customers.

The J. M. Smucker Company

- Rules were set in place to regulate personal and vendor relationships which were not based on our people's basic beliefs. When you put too many rules in place, does it leave the message that we are not trusting people to do the right thing?
- Promotion of less than desirable person to higher level within the company. Results very negative and led to separation.
- Would probably be something on a day-to-day job-related basis and involve ethics—the employee places himself before the company—taking office supplies home, taking a sick day when not really sick ... things that hurt the company but are not readily visible....

None of these survey examples would make the news. Many of the situations occurred down in the bowels of the organization. In small ways, they probably occur frequently every day in almost any organization. No one knows the magnitude and the total costs in lost productivity, frustration, and real dollars from such beliefs breakdowns. My guess is that this total cost is probably greater than that of all the major published examples cited previously.

These four companies have exerted time and effort to make their basic beliefs work. I am sure that most of the companies in the previously cited examples have beliefs and wonder why they didn't work. Business will never be a perfect world. But increasing the effectiveness of your beliefs process will prevent breakdowns from growing to reputation-destroying size and reduce the incidence of small, day-to-day glitches.

Most of these companies have clear, long-term strategic directions and efficient operations to get them to their goals. Corporate, division, and business unit executives put considerable time and effort into seeing that product, market, capability, and result strategies are in place. Managers, supervisors, team leaders, staff groups, professionals, and nonmanagerial salaried and hourly employees see that operational plans and actions to carry out the strategic vision are as effective and productive as possible. That's as it should be. But the "large" and "small" troubles presented were not the result of breakdowns in strategic vision or operational effectiveness. They arose from a failure to understand or get the most from basic beliefs.

SUMMARY

My own consulting experience over the past thirty years strongly supports the need to strengthen basic beliefs. Ben Tregoe and I developed a process to help Kepner-Tregoe clients improve how they formulate and implement strategy.[28] Some of the organizations we worked with already had written creeds, mission statements, or belief statements. Often these were written in uplifting but very general language. For other organizations, the pre-session survey that the CEO and staff completed seemed to be the force for acknowledging the beliefs and stating them. We helped them use beliefs as critical input for formulating product, customer, and capability strategy. We made their basic beliefs a preamble to and part of their statements of strategy. We had them test their strategic conclusions against their beliefs to make sure they were mutually supportive. I don't recall many clients realizing the unique importance of beliefs to strategic efforts. With hindsight, I saw that the time allotted to seek, consolidate, and clarify their basic beliefs was too compressed, and the connection between beliefs and competitive advantage was not made strongly enough. In our early strategic efforts with clients, it bothered Ben and me that too often we saw the beliefs as more important than the client did. We did much to change that along the way. Ultimately, that led to this book.

In this global and fast-changing world, the quality of the products and services you provide and the development and care of the customers you serve are the keys to both short-term success and long-term growth and stability. Whether you are a worker on the line, a salesperson in the field, an individual contributor, a project or team leader, a manager, an executive, or the CEO, your decisions and actions impact the products or services you provide and the customers you serve. Those decisions and actions are guided by your ability to think and by your skill and knowledge. But the level of excellence of those decisions and actions is strongly influenced by the beliefs you apply and the consistency with which you apply them.

Regardless of your level or function, are you aware of and do you understand your company's corporate beliefs? Do those beliefs guide your key decisions and actions? When you see decisions and actions made that run counter to those beliefs, do you act in any way to correct them? Do those in positions of responsibility personify basic beliefs? Do you see meaningful recognition given to those who live by those beliefs and appropriate discipline imposed on those who don't? Do your personal values square well with the corporate beliefs? If you don't feel strong positives in thinking about these questions, there is a need for improvement in the basic beliefs process where you work. Your company or work unit or job may be headed for trouble.

The next chapter will cover the power of basic beliefs to fill the needs expressed in this chapter.

THE POWER OF BELIEFS

The world of business is in constant change. It seems to be increasingly revolutionary versus evolutionary. Both strategy (what the business should be) and operations (how to get there) are affected. Both are conditioned by environmental change—technological, economic, social, and political. Strategic or directional decisions are particularly influenced by the new pressures of global competition, the demise of communism, and emerging industrial nations. Operational practices must take into consideration new approaches to how work is accomplished, organized, and managed.

Mike Hammer, in his book *Beyond Reengineering*, suggests a new, big-picture paradigm as to how work is accomplished: "… horizontal, end-to-end processes like new product development, order fulfillment, and customer management—should become the permanent armature on which work is hung, not just the focus of one-shot improvements…. Unlike the tasks a department manages, those that constitute a process need not be similar: For example, order fulfillment includes selling, credit analysis, picking and packing, and shipping…. Hammer is superb at describing what's in it—and not in it—for people. In it are autonomy and responsibility—elements that … will lead to the professionalization even of blue-collar work. All workers are expected to do whatever it takes to deliver value to a customer, and 'a professional is someone who is responsible for achieving a result rather than performing a task.' Not in it are job promotions, for even giant companies will need just 100 or so process owners. The ranks of managers will dissolve into cadres of professionals."[1] Whatever part of Hammer's work world comes to pass, it is clear that decentralization, employee empowerment, and project team management are here to stay.

There is extensive evidence that the practice of basic beliefs, combined with a simple statement of fundamental purpose, has allowed some companies to adapt to these kinds of changes and sustain growth and success over long periods of time. Basic beliefs are consistently applied to strategic and operational decisions, and that keeps these organizations on top of change and out in front over time.

James Collins and Jerry Porras in *Built to Last* report research that strongly supports this conclusion. They identified eighteen public companies which they called "visionary" based on their success and uniqueness in their industries over a long period of time. They chose contrasting, less successful companies in each industry and looked for differences. The only distinctive characteristics of the visionary companies were a small set of unique core values that had always been in place and applied, and a brief statement of the organizations' purpose or fundamental reason for existence. Given this conclusion, the authors state: "A visionary company carefully preserves and protects its ideology, yet all the specific manifestations of its core ideology must be open for change and evolution."[2] For example, a belief in "rewards and compensation for performance" is changing from an historical individual focus to a team or work unit focus. I found Collins and Porras' research thorough and in full support of their conclusion. If you want to move up the "visionary ladder," their book is recommended.

Companies that sustain the highest growth in respect and profitability over long periods of time have a competitive advantage that goes much deeper than more typical definitions, including:

- a unique feature or benefit in their product or service;
- a unique relationship with their customer base;

- excellence in a capability (technology, production, etc.) that allows them to dominate a product or customer segment;
- financial and business acumen that allows them to bring companies together and produce value beyond the combined total of their separate worth.

This competitive advantage extends far beyond one unique product, one set of loyal customers, or a single technological breakthrough. It carries success far beyond the founders or a particular CEO. These companies have found and kept their basic beliefs. They apply them to every strategic and operational decision that affects the product, customer, capability, or financial result.

If you are part of a "visionary company," you have proven the point about beliefs to yourself and will stay with them. It would make interesting research to examine companies that over time have bounced up and down in terms of success. My hypothesis is that if they determined their basic beliefs, their success bounced up when they applied the beliefs and fell down when they didn't. I used the word "determined" as I believe, along with Collins and Porras, that any ongoing company finds and formulates beliefs from its history. Beliefs are more than just a motto.

The following examples describe companies and their investors, customers, and employees who buy into the power of basic beliefs to influence sustained success. Four examples illustrate what can make the power of beliefs work.

IT TAKES ONE GOOD MAN

There is no better example of the connection between the power of beliefs and sustained results and reputation than Sam Walton and Wal-Mart. Sam Walton relates: "As I look back ..., I realize that ours is a story about the kinds of traditional principles that made America great in the first place. It is a story about entrepreneurship, and risk, and hard work, and knowing where you want to go and being willing to do what it takes to get there. It's a story about believing in your idea even when maybe some other folks don't, and about sticking to your guns. But I think more than anything it proves there's absolutely no limit to what plain, ordinary working people can accomplish if they're given the opportunity and the encouragement and the incentive to do their best. Because that's how Wal-Mart became Wal-Mart: ordinary people joined together to accomplish extraordinary things. At first, we amazed ourselves. And before too long, we amazed everybody else, especially folks who thought America was just too complicated and sophisticated a place for this sort of thing to work anymore."[3]

Walton learned that financial incentives for performance did motivate, but added: "Plenty of companies offer some kind of profit sharing but share absolutely no sense of partnership with their employees because they don't really believe those employees are important, and they don't work to lead them."

There is a feeling of homespun, small-town pride in his success, but he says: "... a smart, motivational, good manager can work what some outsiders call Wal-Mart magic with folks anywhere." Part of his concept of partnership and openness is "... empowering our associates by running the business practically as an open book.... Another important ingredient ... from the very beginning has been our very unusual willingness to share most of the numbers of our business with all the associates. It's the only way they can possibly do their jobs to the best of their abilities—to know what's going on in their business."

Profit is a part of partnership: "If we, as managers, truly dedicate ourselves to instilling that thrill of merchandising— the thrill of buying and selling something at a profit—into every single one of our associate-partners, nothing can ever stop us.

"... [O]ne simple thing that puts it all together: appreciation. All of us like praise. So what we try to practice in our company is to look for things to praise. Look for things that are going right. We want to let our folks know when they are doing something outstanding, and let them know they are important to us.

"You can't praise something that's not done well. You can't be insincere. You have to follow up on things that aren't done well. There is no substitute for being honest with someone and letting them know they didn't do a good job. All of us profit from being corrected—if we're corrected in a positive way. But there's no better way to keep someone doing things the right way than by letting him or her know how much you appreciate their performance. If you do that one simple thing, human nature will take it from there.... Executives who hold themselves aloof from their associates, who won't listen to their associates when they have a problem, can never be true partners with them.... So, as big as we are, we have really tried to maintain an open-door policy at Wal-Mart."

And the results: "Just fifteen years ago the market value of the company was around $135 million; today over $50 billion. But here's a better way to look at it: let's say you bought 100 shares back in that original public offering for $1,650, ... it would have been worth right around $3 million [1992]."[4]

IT TAKES PATIENCE

William M. Gibson, CEO of Manugistics Inc., a computer software and services firm, put it this way: "The greatest challenge [in establishing our culture] was definitely the cynicism of those workers who had become disillusioned by other organizations that said one thing and did another. There was a slight initial reaction that the Elements of Excellence [basic beliefs] were corny. We needed to have the perseverance and the patience to act in a consistent fashion throughout the years to build credibility. As workers begin to see that the company is committed to doing good things, they begin to say, 'I can trust this organization: it will honor the Elements of Excellence; I'm allowed to believe in these philosophies.' You have to be prepared to answer the same questions repeatedly as people struggle to test and validate the sincerity of the organization and its leadership. There are no quick fixes; you have to have the patience and conviction to stand these tests, especially in moments of crisis. You can't blink and divert from the principles you've established or you lose the credibility you've worked so hard to gain."[5]

IT TAKES TOUGHNESS

Levi Strauss ... "is struggling mightily, though not always successfully, to live up to a singular, lofty vision of how to run a modern corporation." CEO Robert D. Haas, a dedicated believer in the power of basic beliefs, "is out to make each of his workers, from the factory floor on up, feel as if they are an integral part of the making and selling of blue jeans.... [a]ll views on all issues—no matter how controversial—are heard and respected. The chairman won't tolerate harassment ... won't do business with suppliers who violate Levi's strict standards regarding work environment and ethics.... 'We are not doing this because it makes us feel good—although it does. We are not doing this because it is politically correct. We are doing this because we believe in the interconnection between liberating the talents of our people and business success.'"[6]

IT TAKES SIMPLICITY

Sears bounced up for a long time and then, for a while, fell downward. Now it is back up through the leadership of CEO Arthur Martinez. Martinez, an outside recruit (former Vice Chairman of Saks Fifth Avenue), was brought in by now-retired CEO Ed Brennan in 1992 when Sears was clearly going down—showing losses of $3.9 billion. Martinez says: "We're replacing 29,000 pages of policies and procedures with two very simple booklets. We call them 'Freedoms' and 'Obligations.' We're trying to tell our managers what they're responsible for, what freedoms they have to make decisions, and where to turn if they need help. But we don't want to codify every possible situation. Part of the trick in getting this company moving again is not dishonoring its past but trying to honor the parts of its past that are relevant to the future. Satisfaction guaranteed, integrity, trust, fair dealing with customers, respect for people are all values that were pretty alive in this organization. They need to be respected."[7]

The next five examples show that the power of beliefs works in many different ways.

IT ALLOWS INDEPENDENCE

Johnson & Johnson's Credo, or basic beliefs, has significant impact far beyond the famous poisoned Tylenol issue. J&J "is performing a juggling act that defies gravity. It runs no fewer than 33 major lines of business, with an astounding 168 operating companies in 53 countries.... If ever a company's top brass could make a case for tightly controlling everything from headquarters in New Jersey, it's Johnson & Johnson.... They don't. Instead, they operate with deliberately redundant operations and amazingly independent management, all held together by a curious system of ethics called the Credo, which places profits and stockholders dead last." And the results: J&J has had steady growth in sales and earnings. It has never lost money since it went public in 1944. Investors have more than doubled their money in the past five years.[8] Former J&J CEO James Burke says: "As a 33% return on stockholders' equity suggests, the Credo turns out to be pretty practical. Because the Credo de-emphasized profits, ... managers are freer to operate long-term. They are not so worried about making mistakes and are under less pressure to cut corners."[9]

IT WORKS ANYWHERE

Listen to these Overseas Chinese capitalists whose bases are predominantly Hong Kong, Singapore, and Taiwan. They have eclipsed Japan as the primary source of capital in the world's fastest growing economy, conservatively estimated at $2 trillion in liquid assets. "How do the Asians do it? In a recent study of what it called 'The East Asian Miracle,' the World Bank turned up no magic formula, no single set of government policies. The key, its experts concluded, is culture.

"... [T]hey have much to teach outsiders about how to build, manage, and sustain fast-growing businesses. Start with values. Regardless of where they live or how rich they are, the Overseas Chinese share an abiding belief in hard work, strong family ties, frugality and education. Yes, this same constellation of virtues defines much of what Westerners have labeled the Protestant ethic, but for the Overseas Chinese these attributes aren't musty relics from their culture's past but compelling rules to live by.... The most treasured asset of any ethnic Chinese businessman, be he a billionaire or a small manufacturer with a one-room workshop, is XINYONG, which means having both a good reputation and a solid credit rating."[10]

ITS REACH IS FAR

Starbucks Coffee Company and its CEO Howard Schultz are stirring up a most ambitious brew: "It is our goal to be the most recognized and respected brand of coffee in the world by the end of the decade. But, "Schultz adds carefully, "we will do it in a way that is compatible with our value system and guiding principles, all of which will be executed against a consistent strategy of building the equity of our brand and maintaining our leadership position."

Here is the way that value system is applied: "Starbucks is the largest corporate donor to Atlanta-based CARE, an international development and relief organization. Schultz earmarks Starbucks' contributions mostly to coffee-producing countries such as Ethiopia, Indonesia, Kenya, and Guatemala. It also sells several CARE-related products in most of its coffee stores. 'We've been involved with them for almost four years,' says Schultz of the partnership with CARE. 'That's so we can give back to the growing regions of the world where we buy coffee. The CARE association is one we are extremely proud of.' ... Schultz was honored last year by the Business Enterprise Trust for 'combining innovative management with social outreach.'"[11]

While Starbucks is not yet a "visionary company" as defined by Collins and Porras, with that focus on basic beliefs Schultz may just make his decade goals and begin to join those visionary ranks over the long term.

IT OVERCOMES CATASTROPHE

Aaron Feuerstein, CEO of Malden Mills, has principles. He has ethical beliefs about people and the community. He has merit beliefs about the customer and the long term. They showed when a massive fire nearly destroyed his manufacturing plant in northern Massachusetts. He continued to pay his 3,000 idle employees, at a cost of many millions of dollars, while the plant was rebuilt.

"I [Michael Ryan, article author] asked Feuerstein, 70, what set him apart from other CEOs. 'The fundamental difference is that I consider our workers an asset, not an expense.' [He later added:] 'I have a responsibility to the workers, both blue-collar and white-collar. I have an equal responsibility to the community. It would have been unconscionable to put 3,000 people on the streets and deliver a death blow to the cities of Lawrence and Methuen.'"[12]

But he was neither foolish—some would have taken the insurance money and run or used the opportunity to move offshore—nor a saint. He is a shrewd businessman who understands the relationships between people's beliefs and their impact on loyalty, creativity, productivity, and long-term sustained growth: "The way to do that is to create so much value that your customers wouldn't dream of looking for another supplier. Indeed, the idea is to build a value creation system of superior products, service, teamwork, productivity, and co-operation with the buyer.... Reduced to its essence, ... as

Feuerstein can tell you, it means superior employees. The correlation between loyal customers and loyal employees is no coincidence."

And the results: "… customer retention at Malden Mills runs roughly 95% which is world class. Employee retention runs above 95%.… As for productivity, from 1982 to 1995, revenues in constant dollars more than tripled while the work force barely doubled. Compare that with an overall productivity increase for the U.S. of a little better than 1% per year.… [I]t's the considered and historically successful policy of a genial manufacturing genius who might serve as a model for every man and woman in business."[13]

IT TURNS THINGS AROUND

At the Jacksonville Electric Authority, Royce Lyles built a new culture by dramatically changing beliefs about people from a dictatorial management style based on crisis control to one that encouraged, measured, and rewarded suggestions and input: "Lyles and his lieutenants generated a stream of programs encouraging productive change. Employee suggestions were solicited aggressively. A successful suggestion meant cash. Ten percent of money saved went as a bonus to the author." One suggestion saved $1 million a year. "Astonished, he [Lyles] heard that 'everyone' had long known it could be done. 'If everybody knew it, why didn't we ever do it?' he asked. The answer trailed back into the long night—of subtropical shambles, orders barked at the slaves, casual dilapidation. The drawl from Frostproof [Florida] sums up that past: 'A culture where you just do what you're told.'

"Lyles' culture changes defy enumeration. Dashboard computers in the trouble trucks, chain routing of meter readers, service crew reorganization, automated recordkeeping, rotating training, tagging of improvements to dollar bonuses, privatization of some processes while still others were being de-privatized and brought in-house."

Here, in summary, is what he accomplished: "Lyles was managing director of JEA from 1979 to 1995. It might not seem the most likely post from which to heal a city's soul. Yet Lyles' tenure flipped a giant switch in the communal mind. What had been the costliest electric utility rates in the state were converted under Lyles into the lowest rates in the state, and some of the lowest in the nation. The once-hated, hide-bound JEA climbed to be ranked by Standard & Poor's as the single most efficient publicly-owned electric utility in America. An old sore spot became a new point of pride."[14]

The last three examples show that the power of beliefs influences many stakeholders.

INVESTORS

Institutional investors are becoming increasingly concerned with a company's practice of its basic beliefs in support of its performance. These investors control $10.8 trillion and hold 20 percent of all the financial assets in the United States. On June 15, 1994, the Board of Directors of CalPERS ($80-billion California Public Employees' Retirement System) decided to consider corporate workplace practices as one criterion for pension investments. This decision was made in part as a result of a study they commissioned from the Gordon Group. This study found that companies using such practices traded at a premium and outperformed the S&P 500 by 16 percent from 1990 to 1994. Companies with poor records of investing in human resources had substandard market valuations and performance. CalPERS is now formally developing measures for its own internal review process.

A balance sheet tells us a lot about financial health, "[B]ut balance sheets do not capture other aspects of a company's performance that are often more important indicators of long-term performance, including the quality and loyalty of the company's work force, the level of investment in training and retraining, the strategies for protecting worker health and safety, and the ca-

pacity of the work force to continually innovate and adapt....
CalPERS' decision to evaluate employee relations issues in its
investment processes is the most important and visible manifestation of two powerful undercurrents in social investing today.
Like many trends starting in California, it provides a glimpse of
things to come, of a new world in which the social construct we
call the publicly traded corporation will increasingly live."[15]

CUSTOMERS

The end-user or customer is also concerned with an organization's beliefs. There is now some empirical proof for the often-
stated maxim, "Do well by doing good." A six-month study by
Walker Research of 1,037 American households concluded:

- "Thirty-five percent say they always or frequently avoid buying a product or service from a business that is perceived as
  unethical.

- Fifty percent say they would not buy, regardless of any dis-
  count, from a company that is not socially responsible.

- Twenty-six percent of potential investors said business practices and ethics are extremely important in determining
  where to invest.

- ... [T]hree-fourths of the sample already is refusing to buy
  from one or more companies ... poor service being cited 52%
  of the time ... dubious business practices ranking a close
  second among 48%.

    From a list of 74 suggested attributes, respondents checked
20 most often [used] as indicators of a company's social conscience.... Lumping all those characteristics together, respondents ranked them in the following order in determining a
company's sense of corporate social responsibility: (1) business
practices, (2) community support, (3) employee treatment, (4)
quality, (5) environment, (6) service, (7) price, (8) convenience
and (9) stability."[16]

EMPLOYEES

Where people choose to work is influenced by the organization's beliefs. A study by John Sheridan at the University of Alabama at Birmingham makes this point. The study covered retention rates of 904 college grads at six international accounting firms with offices in a single large western city. Choosing one city controlled for differing regional labor-market conditions. Three of the firms (labeled A) had a culture or beliefs emphasizing the interpersonal relationship values of team orientation and respect for people. Two firms (labeled B) had a culture emphasizing work-task values of detail and stability. The A firm hires stayed 14 months longer than B firm hires. Using many statistics, the article calculates the opportunity lost by B versus A was $6 to $9 million. A word of caution: These are high-mobility firms. Results elsewhere may be different.[17]

The following quote from *Fortune*'s Corporate Reputation Evaluation summarizes the unique nature of basic beliefs as the key to a company's being most admired and successful over time: "As a company navigates this roiling sea of change without the old buoys of hierarchy and supervision, the constellations of beliefs and values that make up its culture reemerge as the stars to steer by." Procter & Gamble's CEO Edwin Artzt says it practically: "What's critical is a company's ability to perform successfully across generations of management. That requires a culture that can be passed down from generation to generation."[18]

Roberto C. Goizueta, CEO of The Coca-Cola Company and *Chief Executive* magazine's 1996 Man of the Year, describes one way to pass culture down: "What kind of person do you envision as your successor? 'He or she must have energy; intellectual character; integrity; an inquisitive, innovative mind; determination; a sense of purpose; and an engaging personality. He or she must be able to fulfill the CEO's three key responsibilities: being ultimately accountable to stakeholders, employees, cities, and society for company growth, character, and perpetuation; providing moral, ethical, and dynamic leadership; and deciding what and when to delegate. Everything starts from there.'" These beliefs and his leadership have guided Coca-Cola to enviable heights: an increase in net annual income from $482 million in 1981 to almost $3 billion in 1995; growth in worldwide soft drink market share from 37 percent to 47 percent in the same period; a share price at a compound annual 26 percent growth rate, creating almost $85 billion in shareholder wealth.[19]

SUMMARY

The direct impact of beliefs on short- and long-term corporate growth and profitability has long been debated. On the plus side, Jim Burke, former Chairman of Johnson & Johnson, believed strongly in J&J's credo. "To prove his point, he commissioned a study of the financial performance of U.S. companies that have had a written value statement for at least a generation. The net income of those 20 companies increased by a factor of 23 during a period when the GNP grew by a factor of 2½."[20]

On the minus side, a recent article quotes Ken Roberts, CEO of the consulting firm Lippincott & Margulies: "I am not aware of any real quantitative link between the use of mission statements [which include basic beliefs] and financial performance." The article goes on to say, "The bottom line: Mission statements may improve corporate performance, and they may not."[21]

I am sure that in evaluating corporate success one cannot make a truly "quantitative link" between any one practice and its specific impact on overall results. Over time successful results are a blend of focused strategy, highly effective day-to-day operations, and the application of enduring beliefs.

In the past, basic beliefs often were thought of as nice to have but not essential to business success. Printed statements of beliefs were often hung on the wall and placed in the new employee handbook; they were good for press releases, media coverage, advertising slogans, or use at the annual meeting or in the annual report. But everyone knew the reality: Get the stuff out at all costs, listen to the boss, look out for yourself, and don't stir up trouble when you see things going wrong. Those days are gone!

Robert Haas, CEO at Levi, recalls a disturbing distinction from the past: "Levi has always treated people fairly and cared about their welfare. The usual term is 'paternalism.' But it is more than paternalism, really—a genuine concern for people and a recognition that people make this business successful.

"In the past, however, that tradition was viewed as something separate from how we ran the business. We always talked about the 'hard stuff' and the 'soft stuff.' The soft stuff was the company's commitment to our workforce. And the hard stuff was what really mattered: getting pants out the door.

"What we've learned is that the soft stuff and the hard stuff are becoming increasingly intertwined. A company's values—what it stands for, what its people believe in—are crucial to its competitive success. Indeed, values drive the business."[22]

Senior management at EDS (Electronic Data Systems) agrees: "He [CEO Les Alberthal] seems almost superstitiously concerned that EDS no longer function the way it did in the Perot days, when one man made virtually every major decision.... Explains Fernandes [vice-chairman Gary Fernandes]: 'We've moved from a cult of personality to a culture where the emphasis is on teams arriving at collective decisions.' ... Starting in 1994, Alberthal began putting every EDS manager, starting with himself, through an extraordinary series of training sessions that delve deeply into the realm of feelings, aiming to stimulate greater sensitivity to customers, employees, and colleagues. About half of EDS's 12,000 managers have received the training so far.... They're not listening to feelings for fun; they're doing it because that's where the money is. Says Dean Linderman, an Alberthal confidant who supervises leadership development: 'In an organization with a history of avoidance of the soft stuff, the heart-and-soul stuff, we've now said that not only is heart and soul important, but it's a prerequisite to take the corporation where we want to go.'"[23]

If you haven't fully connected your soft stuff basic beliefs with your hard stuff—how the business gets run—it's time. If you have given considerable thought to your basic beliefs and have a process that guides both long- and short-term decision making, then you need only to fine tune and sharpen it. If you have stated basic beliefs but are uncertain as to their impact, you need to review the communication, application, and monitoring of the process. If you haven't given any thought to basic beliefs, get yours out and develop a process to make them work.

Rosabeth Kanter makes the relationship between beliefs and results crystal clear: "Where credos make a difference, the values are appropriate to the business. They fit what the business is trying to achieve; they reflect a theory of the business, a model of its success factors, that clarifies the relationship between its values and economics. Banc One's 'uncommon partnership' philosophy, valuing both local autonomy to serve the customer and shared operating standards to create a unified team, derived from a shrewd understanding of profit drivers and people motivators. Without a theory linking a company's values and economics, any statement of values contributes more to global warming than to competitive advantage; it is just hot air."[24]

With an understanding of the need for beliefs and their power to affect sustained success, let's move into how to improve them through the basic beliefs process.

Basic Beliefs Process	
1. <u>DETERMINE</u>	4. Apply
2. <u>ARTICULATE</u>	5. Reward
3. Communicate	6. Review

C H A P T E R

T H R E E

WHERE THEY COME FROM AND HOW THEY ARE WORDED

The basic beliefs process will provide guidelines to handle these issues:

- Seeking the organization's unique beliefs
- Wording beliefs for clarity and understanding
- Communicating beliefs for commitment and application
- Gaining application of beliefs throughout the organization
- Using recognition to motivate continuing application of beliefs
- Monitoring beliefs for progress and update

Determining the organization's beliefs and then stating them for clear meaning are addressed in this chapter.

Your early "growing up" years and environment shape the beliefs you later bring to the world of work. "I grew up in an environment that imprinted lots of things on me," says Schultz (Howard Schultz, CEO of Starbucks Coffee Company). "One of them was the plight of working-class families. I have never forgotten where I came from. I've wanted to be in a situation where I could effect change by providing respect and dignity. I wanted to provide ownership and the security of health benefits for every employee."[1]

William M. Gibson, CEO of Manugistics: "I attribute part of my philosophies to my early work experiences in blue collar environments. While working in a warehouse and driving a truck during my college years, I learned a lesson that has been reinforced every day of my business career—people don't come to work asking, 'How can I screw up today?' Most people come to work wanting to do some good. If you, as a leader, can create an environment in which people feel that they're being supported and have control of their own success or failure, they'll not only flourish but also step up to any challenge. This principle applies to all levels of the organization. No matter how sophisticated the individual or how many layers of veneer he or she may have developed during the years, there's a real person inside with the same basic needs. I've seen so many managers become demoralized or fail because they've forgotten or lack the understanding of this basic concept."[2]

Our American heritage has made its contribution to the beliefs we build into our companies and jobs. David Vogel writes in *Across the Board*: "Thus, thanks in part to the role played by Reformed Protestantism in defining American values, the United States remains a highly moralistic society. Compared to the citizens of other capitalist nations, Americans are more likely to believe that business and morality are, and should be, related to each other, that good ethics is good business, and that business activity both can and should be consistent with high personal moral values."[3]

The importance I place on trust and honesty as business beliefs, as well as personal beliefs, was shaped while working in an iron foundry during high school and college. Workers selected a container load of castings from a holding area. They were then packed in forms with sand for annealing. We were paid by the ton. Some loads in the holding area were small castings with compact heavy weight. Others, like clutch pedals, were gangling and light in weight. It would have been easy to cheat by changing load tickets or to be greedy by only choosing high weight/volume loads. But that didn't happen among these tough, hardworking men. I soon learned that they had a very basic code of ethics concerning trust, fairness, and honesty and you didn't violate it. Once you bought into that code, they would do almost anything to help a young student in a man's world. Those values stuck!

WHERE DO BASIC BELIEFS COME FROM?

While top management has a responsibility to see that the company's basic beliefs are developed, the stimulus to initiate or improve beliefs can come from any unit, level, function, or individual in the organization. If you are not aware of any stated and applied beliefs in your company, ask if there are any. If there are only informal beliefs, ask if these are the true beliefs of the company. If there are stated values and they are not being consistently applied or are abused, find a safe way to bring this to light. Review your own values and see how they square with the organization's beliefs. How will you handle any differences?

This example illustrates one way to initiate a search for beliefs: "In 1986, the Manugistics' management team negotiated the purchase of the company from Contel. At that critical juncture, CEO William M. Gibson and his management team felt it was essential to the firm's future success to consult with employees and customers to identify the culture, philosophies and values needed to create and implement the company's mission most effectively.... After several months of surveys and discussion with employees and clients, ... the company formulated the Elements of Excellence which includes these three statements: 1) We treat others as we would like to be treated. 2) Partnership with our clients results in superior products. 3)Team success is more important than personal glory."[4]

So with top management's support, the company's beliefs were identified by employees and customers. Commitment to basic beliefs is much more likely when all levels are involved in the process of determining them.

I do believe it is top management's sole responsibility to see that an effective basic beliefs process is put in place, monitored, and maintained. That process begins with determining beliefs. A *Fortune* article reports that in a study of 161 top executives around the world, of the five distinct leadership styles that emerged, 30 percent featured the "Human Assets Approach" style. Here the CEO manages for success through people, emphasizing teamwork and true empowerment. This is done by designing powerful training systems and coherent programs for measuring performance. It also entails explicitly teaching employees desired values and behaviors, and developing human asset leaders to both empower people to act as CEOs and reward them when they do. Gillette, PepsiCo, and Southwest Airlines follow this primary approach to leadership. "Al Zeien, CEO of Gillette, is the ultimate people manager. He knows an astounding number of his company's 34,000 employees, traveling almost constantly to meet them in groups and alone.... Along with the experience of its global work force, Gillette's success will be based on those managers sharing the same values, values that put the company's earnings before those of a single country or product line."[5]

You have an opportunity to create beliefs from scratch when you start a company and during its formative years. What kinds of ethic and merit beliefs are really going to produce success in this company? Don't sit and make a "do good" wish list. If you're starting a company, buttress your own beliefs by studying successful start-up companies like yours and the beliefs they practice. Initially those beliefs may be informal and unwritten. Then, nurture those few initial beliefs. As best you can, measure their impact on important strategic and operational decisions. Then expand, modify, or add to them in the formative years. At some point you will want to put them in writing.

To illustrate, this is how Chuck Kepner and Ben Tregoe started K-T, the firm with which I spent thirty plus years of my working life. While doing research at the RAND Corporation, they discovered various air force officers finding quite different solutions to the same problem. They wondered why and wanted to continue this research to explore the areas of problem solving and decision making. RAND wasn't interested in this research so Chuck and Ben formed their own company to develop some very fundamental ideas about these processes.

In starting their business Ben and Chuck had two options. They could use their ideas as consultants to recommend solutions to an organization's problem and then walk away until the next problem developed. Or, they could found an educational consultancy and instill those ideas in an organization's employees so the client company could do a better job of solving its own problems. Either form of business was viable, although very different. As a result of their own independent education and business backgrounds, both men had strong feelings and convictions about the power of education, particularly when it improved thinking ability rather than teaching specific subject matter. Their beliefs led them to develop an educational consultancy, which became the bedrock of the firm's uniqueness, growth, and success.

In its formative years, experience may suggest that a business adopt a new belief to improve its odds for long-term success. K-T began teaching its problem solving and decision making ideas in a seminar format. Participants practiced the ideas in a simulated company. Often, these were "public sessions" with many clients in attendance. Our focus was on leading participants to an understanding of the ideas. To us, as educators, it was stimulating and fun. When we followed up with clients to talk with past participants about the experience, we found that they had fond memories of the program, but there was little evidence of application on the job. We had assumed that if we taught the ideas well, behaviors would change and on-the-job application of the ideas would follow. Wrong!

We soon added this merit belief statement to K-T's list: "Produce useful, practical results for each client." This caused us to focus our work internally with a client company, agreeing on objectives for a work group and structuring the learning to accomplish those objectives. We added time to the seminar and participants spent that time applying the ideas we taught to their real on-the-job problems and decisions. That step provided a practical bridge to the real world and motivated behavior change by demonstrating results. The new belief statement played a key role in our survival and growth. K-T continues to broaden its application of that belief.

If you work in an organization that's been around awhile and now want to formalize basic beliefs, or improve those that are in practice, you have a rich history through which to search. No doubt the original founders started with their ethic and merit beliefs. IBM's three simple values came down from Tom Watson: "Give full consideration to the individual employee; spend a lot of time making customers happy; go the last mile to do a thing right."[6]

Your employees, customers, suppliers, and competitors are all great sources for identifying beliefs. They can say very explicitly what your beliefs are in practice. New employees, not yet "brainwashed," are excellent sources for critique and verification.

Gathering or sharpening basic beliefs can be done in several ways. One effective format is a project team reporting to the CEO. That team can include a cross-section of employees from every level and function. The CEO may be a member of the team or may just review its work. Either way, beliefs application will not work without the CEO's commitment and support.

Conoco's EVP, Gary Edwards, provides another approach: "'The process needs to cascade down to the individual departments, to the employees themselves.' Everyone who is going to live with the statement should get his 2 cents in. Edwards first brought his managing directors together. 'We identified the values we felt were important. We basically brainstormed for half a day. Then I asked groups further down to do the same thing. We found threads of consistency. On the core values we got quick agreement.'"[7]

In other organizations, it is the CEO who leads the charge to lay out and state the organization's beliefs. He or she seeks input from and then tests conclusions with key executive staff. This approach is positive because basic beliefs are supported by, committed to, and ingrained in the key decision makers. But this approach may cause difficulty in that commitment and credibility may be lacking, as employees down the line have no part in the formation process.

Regardless of what structure you use when forming or sharpening your beliefs, the following is sound advice from Thomas A. Stewart writing in *Fortune*: "Values don't sprout in the CEO's office or the HR department; they don't bloom on organizational trellises—the armature of boundaries and lines where the company ends and the world begins. They grow out of core professional skills, communities of practice [an informal group of people who have a shared interest in a subject]. Here, as everywhere in business, formal organization matters less. We're flat, fluid, networked, virtual; we're an adhocracy; we work in projects and cross-functional teams. If this is where we live, this is where we will find our values. They grow where all the ladders start: in the work, not the organization chart."[8]

When identifying basic beliefs, don't worry initially about the ultimate wording. Get the ideas down on paper. Seek both ethic and merit beliefs. If you are starting from scratch, the initial list may be long. Then the tough task of boiling the list down to the true beliefs must be accomplished. These are the beliefs that have produced success or excellence over long periods of time. Check major strategic and operational decisions that were highly successful to see what beliefs were applied. Also review decisions that failed to see which beliefs weren't applied. The final list will be short—a half-dozen or so beliefs that have stood the test of time.

HOW BASIC BELIEFS ARE WORDED

Stating beliefs so that they can be applied is not easy work. Tim Smucker, chairman of the company that bears his family name, says: "The most difficult part of setting strategy was putting our basic beliefs down on paper. They are very deeply felt, and we wanted to be sure to dot every 'i' and cross every 't.' The essence of what we believe was not too difficult to identify, but describing our beliefs in a document was a real challenge."[9]

Beliefs must be specific enough to guide decision making and behavior. Ethic beliefs about honesty or equality are clear in intent. Merit beliefs about people, such as empowerment or participation, receive further definition as they are translated into policies, procedures, practices, and behavior. Other belief statements are very specific and include standards within them:

- 3M—"Innovation; 'Thou shalt not kill a new product idea'"
- Boeing—"Being on the leading edge of aeronautics technology; being pioneers"
- GE—"To become #1 or #2 in every market we serve"
- Merck—"Science-based innovation, not imitation"[10]

Barnett Banks' belief about the level of its reputation is clear: "We are Barnett, the nationally recognized standard in the financial services industry." The J. M. Smucker Company's belief about the quality of products sets a clear standard: "Smucker's will be the highest quality products offered in our industry." The American Automobile Association's belief about its services and products provides clear guidance for its actions: "AAA services and products will be tested, proved practical and reliable, and offered only to add value to membership."

Two of K-T's merit beliefs are generic, yet they are specific enough to have guided the firm's strategic and operational focus from its early beginnings. The first has not changed over the years. It reads, "Transfer our ideas to the client, enabling them to do for themselves, rather than do for them." This belief has kept K-T focused on improving ways to instill rational thinking in any client organization. It also discouraged us from engaging in more generalized consulting such as solving problems for a client. When we worked with a client to solve a major problem, it was at the client's request and only done to support this belief. It expresses the classic advice, "Teach them to fish" versus "Give them a fish."

The second K-T merit belief that has broadened in application over the years reads: "Value a workforce diverse in experience, education, background, and culture." We fully staff each of our international companies with nationals of the country or area involved. We consciously hire professionals with diverse backgrounds and work experience. Women professionals abound, and they participate in all management levels. In Japan, working female professionals are not a part of the culture. Yet K-T employs female professionals in its Japanese offices; that demonstrates the power of this belief.

There are many ways to state basic beliefs. K-T's are expressed in a series of short, discrete clauses. For example: "Continuously improve the quality of our services, our client relationships, and our company's operations." Some companies use just a few simple words. This example from Barnett Bank's Operating Vision illustrates: "We help each other succeed." Harley-Davidson provides another example: "Respect the individual."

Each of J. M. Smucker's beliefs has been expanded into a paragraph to show how it will be manifested in their strategic direction and operational practices. For example, on their belief about quality: "Quality applies to our products, our manufacturing methods, our marketing efforts, our people, and our relationships with each other. We will only produce and sell products that enhance the quality of life and well-being. These will be the highest quality products offered in our respective markets because Smucker's growth and business success have been built on quality. We will continuously look for ways to achieve daily improvements that will, over time, result in consistently superior products and performance. At Smucker's, quality comes first. Sales growth and earnings will follow."

The American Automobile Association provides a similar example in its belief about community and country: "We will be good corporate neighbors, engaging in public service consistent with our mission, the needs of members, the communities we serve and the national interest. In pursuing public policy positions, AAA will remain objective and responsible, relying on our credibility, expertise and research in public policy formulation."

The Cooper Tire and Rubber Company statement gives the origin of its three simple beliefs phrases and then expands on what they mean. "It was in 1926 that I. J. Cooper expressed our Company's Business Creed with these words: 'It wouldn't be called a plan or a policy by a high-powered modern business expert because it is not complicated enough. In fact, it is very simple. Our platform has only three planks in it: Good Merchandise, Fair Play, and a Square Deal. Good merchandise because it doesn't pay to make, sell, or use an inferior article. Fair prices that satisfy the user, leave the dealer with a profit and the maker with a margin to cover his labor, thought, and investment. And a square deal to everyone, every time, because you can't beat a natural law and still progress and prosper.' These words were true then, are true today, and will remain true tomorrow."[11]

Mission statements usually articulate basic beliefs and may include a short description of fundamental purpose: "Dexter Corporation is to be recognized as an important and environmentally responsive specialty materials company that derives superior growth and returns from quality products and responsive services based on proprietary technology and operating excellence that provides genuine benefit to customers worldwide, rewards talented and dedicated employees, and satisfies shareholder expectations."[12]

These kinds of beliefs have guided these organizations' success in the past and will do so in the future. Their basic intent and meaning will not change, but their interpretation in policies, procedures, systems, and operating practices through which they are applied must be reviewed and modified regularly. Seeing that this happens is a good function for a basic beliefs officer or committee or a beliefs project team reporting to the CEO.

Getting beliefs to say exactly what you mean and stating them in a way that anyone can easily understand requires some work. Too often this doesn't happen: "Unfortunately, most mission statements are written in Corporatese. Professors James C. Collins and Jerry I. Porras of the Stanford University Graduate School of Business have studied corporate vision the way car mechanics study transmissions. They learned that one of the things a mission statement must do is inspire, and if it is to inspire it must speak to readers in such a way that it galvanizes them. At its chestiest, Corporatese would not galvanize any creature outside of the legal department."[13]

"Galvanizing" and getting out of "Corporatese" happens when people in all levels of the organization who must live with the finished product are involved in or review the writing. Finding just the right words to describe a belief takes discussion and thought: "CEO Skip LeFauve of Saturn played wordsmith and felt his time was well spent. He and Saturn's employees considered making 'commitment to customer satisfaction' Saturn's No. 1 value. After much discussion, however, they changed it to 'customer enthusiasm.' Says LeFauve: 'We decided satisfaction was just business as usual. Enthusiasm raised the bar.'

"At ME International, workers are hammering out a statement of their own right now, with help from Rob Lebow, consultant and president of the Lebow Co. in Bellevue, Washington. Subjected to much noodling, here is how one value has evolved: First draft—Inspire active participation in the growth of the business to benefit everyone. Second draft—Inspire active participation in the growth of everyone to benefit the business. Third draft—Inspire active participation in the growth of everyone to benefit our business. A waste of time? Not to them."[14] This kind of involvement and effort produces a level of reality, understanding, and commitment that is hard to get any other way.

Having a belief and then stating it so vaguely that misguided self-interest can easily find a way around it debases and destroys the purpose. This says: On paper I want to appear upstanding, but in practice I do whatever I want.

A congressional example well illustrates this point. "An extensive *Business Week* review of financial disclosure filings by members of Congress reveals that many elected officials or their relatives routinely invest in or even actively trade stocks in industries under congressional scrutiny or about which they have special knowledge. Under current law, members are only required to disclose their investments and transactions, as well as those of their immediate families, once a year. Even then, the disclosures are in broad dollar ranges. None of this activity is illegal, but critics say the current rules give members too much opportunity to profit from their positions. 'The ethics rules are so vague that members can say that what they are doing is not specifically prohibited,' says Michael A. Calabrese, a director of the public interest group Congress Watch.... Congressional ethics rules place virtually no restrictions on investments by members. They require members to disclose their investments and transactions every year. The only strict prohibition bars members from voting on or pushing legislation that benefits a very small group that includes themselves. But if the bill benefits them as members of a larger group—as shareholders, for example,—they face no restrictions."[15]

Such charades influence one's reputation far beyond that belief. No wonder Congress is held in such low overall esteem. But this vagueness occurs in the business world as well. Organizations that espouse a belief like "treating employees fairly"—without including any descriptions of what "fairly" means—can end up with top executives walking away with million-dollar golden parachutes while downsized employees get a few weeks of severance pay.

The following are the overall categorized responses to the essay question in our beliefs survey:

"How would you suggest your company's basic beliefs be improved as far as changing or adding to how they are currently stated?"

CATEGORY	RESPONSES	PERCENT
No change—just use them	197	55
More concise or specific	39	11
Change wording or intent	56	15
Miscellaneous	67	19

Typical comments from within the various categories suggest that testing the wording of basic beliefs from time to time is a good practice.

Category—No Change—Just Use Them

• I don't think they should be changed. The Basic Beliefs as stated reflect high ideals of what the company should strive for. I feel they are important in a time in our society when business ethics have been declining and many other companies are scrambling to formulate programs of ethics and quality.

Category—More Concise or Specific

• The basic belief statement is written using words that represent hard to measure values. Consequently, many people I talk to do not remember the statement because it does not stick out by stating more specific degrees of values.

• Simplify—less words.

• Clarify or expound more on "ethics."

• The beliefs speak to the quality of products and services ... more specific in terms of how these products and services are delivered ... when and how the customer chooses.

Category—Change Wording or Intent

• More definition on how we improve the lives of our customers.

• Expand the statement to where employees can recognize actions and behaviors in the statement.

- Relate basic beliefs realistically to today's business environment—fewer "blue sky" statements—more realistic interpretation.
- Add something about rewards for behavior and action supporting basic beliefs.
- Yes—change "empowerment" to "enable" or enabling; very confusing—in many cases, most management has been "micro" style—when people are empowered, micro management simply moves one level down. People need to be *enabled* to perform.

Better testing for understanding and critique of the connection between reality and meaning should be ongoing. As one person replied to this question: "Get out there with the employees. Pick some out of every department and ask them how they (beliefs) could have been made better. Ask them how they would make them better for everyone."

The best summary for this chapter is to take you through the process followed at The American Automobile Association as they determined and stated their basic beliefs. While you must develop your own way, this example will illustrate the level of thinking and effort that must be applied to this part of the process. At AAA, there was a long history of basic beliefs, but this was the first time they were being formalized and written. Obviously, if you already have a formal statement of your basic beliefs and your goal is to sharpen and update that work, your task will be proportionately lighter, but no less critical in importance.

In early 1990, two of AAA's senior corporate executives came to my summer home in Minnesota, and we spent two days defining their development needs and discussing how K-T might help. They were interested in corporate strategy, and we agreed to look at basic beliefs as a starting point. There was much debate on how to go about this. AAA is a federation—it has a corporate headquarters, a corporate board, and a national support staff to provide services to its member Clubs. But each of its 100-plus Clubs has its own corporate structure: a board of directors, a president, and independent operations. Therefore, there was much discussion on who does what, including developing product and customer strategy, policies, and basic beliefs.

We agreed that to strengthen relationships and bring focus to major efforts, we should try for an overall set of corporate beliefs that all could commit to and use. Later, I met with then-CEO Jim Creal to discuss the merits of this approach. He quickly bought into the idea. We talked about his knowledge and feelings on historical AAA beliefs. We discussed the need for a proper balance between the corporate or association function—the "glue" that holds them together—and the needs and requirements of the individual Clubs who serve the members (customers). The importance of serving members and adding value to them through the scope and quality of product offerings was a recurring theme. Jim also described the importance AAA placed on employees and on service to country and community.

I prepared a draft of his thoughts. He reviewed it with key people reporting to him and with other associates, and they made significant modifications. They organized beliefs around Members, the Association, Employees, and Community and Country.

In December 1990 about 150 headquarters' executives and Club CEOs attended AAA's annual Club CEO conference. After a briefing, they broke into five cross-sectional teams and spent the morning debating, discussing, and sharpening the basic beliefs draft. Summaries of team reports were presented to the full group, and those summaries were used to develop the statement of AAA basic beliefs, which will be presented later in this book.

That afternoon the break-out teams met again to test the relevance of what they had accomplished. They discussed certain preselected, long-standing organizational issues and the implication and influence of AAA's newly formalized basic beliefs for resolving them. Among those issues were: minimum product standards, lack of uniformity in Club services, responsibilities for strategic planning at Association or Club level, resource allocation, public policy, and creating more value for members. The time and effort devoted to thinking through, debating, and formally stating their beliefs was instrumental in the teams' ability to discuss and reach a consensus on plans to resolve those issues. The message was clear: Take back to the Association and to each Club the importance of basic beliefs and their influence on strategic and operational issues and decisions.

This part of AAA's basic beliefs process was excellent. Later you will read that in parts of AAA, the communication and application of beliefs broke down and needed to be fixed. One of the purposes of this book is to see that this doesn't happen to other companies. Finally, you will see how, under new leadership, AAA has significantly improved the power of its beliefs as drivers of decision making.

When you have finished initially stating or sharpening your organization's beliefs, select an independent team to test the conclusions. Select the team members from all levels and functions in your organization. Review the beliefs with customers, suppliers, stockholders, and the like. Are these the real beliefs that have made your company successful up to now and that will sustain it in the future?

Now that your beliefs are determined and stated, the next chapter will explore ways they can be communicated for understanding and commitment.

Basic Beliefs Process	
1. Determine	4. Apply
2. Articulate	5. Reward
3. **COMMUNICATE**	6. Review

GETTING OUT THE MESSAGE

Gaining commitment to basic beliefs requires much more than letting everybody know what they are. The letter from the CEO, the card on the desk, the framed posters in the right places, or the general meeting for the unveiling will not do the job fully. These are all one-way driven methods. They can help as reminders, but they won't gain understanding, commitment, or application of the basic beliefs.

Communication is the bridge between the hard work of finding and stating beliefs on one hand, and building them into the lifeblood of the entire organization on the other. Beliefs must be shared across the organization with all employees. Again, there is no one medium through which to accomplish this. But the major communication approaches used must provide for give and take. Each executive, manager, and employee must understand the basic beliefs, the implications of them for his or her job, how they will be measured and monitored, and the rewards for their application and consequences for not using them. To gain the level of commitment required to accomplish this takes interaction, dialogue, and training.

For example, an ethic belief about honesty or a merit belief about quality would seem easy to communicate. We all know what these words mean and most of us want to do a "good job." But for many reasons it is not that easy. Back on the firing line, high and tough goals are a reality. Under pressure, beliefs like honesty or quality can be pushed aside. A violation of beliefs can be self-motivated, result from peer pressure, or may be due to a supervisor who ignores or condones it. A belief about quality may be well understood down on the line, but others who less directly influence quality may be overlooked. Some people don't define honesty the same way when it comes to company matters versus their own. Cultural, social, and ethnic differences can cloud the intent of beliefs. There may be gray areas where compromise between the intent of a belief and another goal may be the best answer. There is also the difficult issue of having to choose between two rights, versus the easier choice of right versus wrong. When a colleague violates a belief, you may experience a conflict between loyalty to your associate and loyalty to the company.

How should these tough issues be handled? It is better to discuss and debate them as part of the communication process rather than just letting them happen with no forethought as to how they might be addressed. There may not be a single, uniform answer for every individual in each situation. But you can encourage employees to think carefully about any problem when it occurs—balancing all of the inputs to arrive at the best possible solution with minimum consequence.

Communication of beliefs should flow through the normal communication channels of the company and its units. For maximum impact and commitment, the manager or supervisor of the work unit should be involved. This lends real credibility and establishes accountability. It allows organizational units to discuss and determine how those beliefs specifically impact and influence their decisions and outputs. Examples relevant to that work unit can be discussed to make sure that tough situations in which beliefs are most likely to be compromised are included. Human resource professionals can be helpful in providing an approach for this process. But in no way should the actual communication of beliefs be delegated to any staff or support group.

At Home Depot, top management stays involved. "Founders Bernard Marcus, CEO, and Arthur Blank, president, continue to lead training sessions even though the company now has 70,000 employees. Says Marcus: 'Nobody else does training this way. It's time consuming, it's hard work.' The CEO is chief training officer? Get used to it. How else do you instill the right culture in a company?"[1] That kind of communication process says it all!

A division of 3-M follows another approach: "In a corporation that strives to be best, creating opportunities for communication is half the battle won. At 3M's dental products division, nonmanagement employees are invited to strategic planning meetings, held town-hall style with the division VP presiding. The process can involve as many as 50 people meeting for three days off-site. The division receives employee satisfaction scores that are 25% higher than the rest of the company. Other parts of the company are adopting this practice."[2] Basic beliefs can be built into this normal communications practice.

CEO Bob Haas of Levi Strauss has an interesting perspective: "One way is to model the new behaviors we are looking for. For example, senior managers try to be explicit about our vulnerability and failings. We talk to people about the bad decisions we've made. It demystifies senior management and removes the stigma traditionally associated with taking risks. We also talk about the limitations of our own knowledge, mostly by inviting other people's perspectives."[3]

The communication of basic beliefs must be an ongoing and continuous effort. At our own company, Ben Tregoe illustrated the influence of our basic beliefs on strategic and operational decisions at every opportunity. As he traveled to each subsidiary abroad, each U.S. region, and at headquarters management and board meetings, basic beliefs were always a part of his review and of any presentation he made. As I traveled around the company, I often found myself focused on our basic beliefs when decisions were made. We didn't bat a thousand; nobody does. But everyone in the company knew our beliefs and the importance they played in the history, in the present, and in the future of our business.

Communicating basic beliefs is also part of day-to-day management and work. There is no better time to instill beliefs than in the one-on-one relationships involved in training and mentoring processes.

The McKinsey consultancy provides a good example: "Its consultants work on teams of mixed rank, and senior people are expected to help junior people along. Part of the development process is quite formal: It is customary for young associates, not partners, to make presentations to clients, for instance, and mentoring is an important criterion in partners' appraisals. But long hours, hard work, and plenty of travel to places like West Moose Lung provide opportunities for teammates to forge personal relationships. 'It's like the old craft apprenticeship system,' says Joel Bleeke, a senior partner whose clients are mostly in financial services. 'The relationship begins as an act of will, not affection, but it becomes much more of an emotional attachment over time. When you are mentoring for leadership, you have to convey much more than problem-solving skills and your personal network—you need to convey aspirations, instill values, excitement, a view that almost anything is possible. You need to instill positive energy.'"[4]

Formal training programs of any kind can play a key role in the ongoing communication of basic beliefs. If the training is participative and has the support and involvement of management, it can be a powerful communicator of basic beliefs no matter the subject of the training. Orientation for new employees should include heavy doses of beliefs. "Ethics training normally begins with orientation sessions and open discussions of the firm's code of ethics. This is often followed by the use of … scenarios which reflect situations that employees may face on the job. This gives employees a chance to make ethical decisions in realistic situations and to discuss these situations openly with peers and supervisors. Organizations such as McDonnell Douglas and General Dynamics have used scenario training to transform their codes of ethics from simple documents to tools for training, education and communication about ethical standards."[5]

New supervisors, team leaders, and managers need training in how to model beliefs and how to communicate and manage the beliefs process in their operation. Robert Haas, Levi Strauss, describes their training: "Another important way to communicate values is through training. We've developed a comprehensive training program that we call the core curriculum. The centerpiece is a week-long course known as 'leadership week' that helps managers practice the behavior outlined in the Aspirations Statement. We run about 20 sessions a year for a small group of about 20 people at a time. By the end of this year, the top 700 people in the company will have been through it. And at least one member of the executive management committee—the top 8 people in the company—or some other senior manager participates in every week-long session, just to send a signal of how important this is to us."[6]

Making beliefs a part of any training sends a very clear message—we got 'em, communicate 'em, and use 'em. "GE happily spends $500 million annually—but don't rely on course work to magically produce leaders. Ultimately the purpose of GE's Crotonville school is to transmit GE's values to employees."[7]

Howard Schultz, Starbucks Coffee Company CEO, calls quality training an art form: "Every employee receives a minimum of 24 hours of classroom training about coffee and about service before they step behind a service counter. Regular on-going follow-up classes are also scheduled. 'The real issue is not the training itself,' he says, 'but combining the training with ownership and health benefits so that the people behind the counter have both a philosophical and financial commitment to the outcome of their actions. In this way, we feel that the value system and the guiding principles of our company have been embraced by our people.'"[8]

As part of an effective ongoing communication program, various representations of basic beliefs help keep them in sight and mind. Innovative approaches help get the message across: "Citicorp has developed an ethics board game, which teams of employees use to solve hypothetical quandaries. General Electric employees can tap into specially designed interactive software on their personal computers to get answers to ethical questions. At Texas Instruments, employees are treated to a weekly column on ethics over an international electronic news service. One popular feature: a kind of Dear Abby mail bag, answers provided by the company's ethics officer, Carl Skoogland, that deals with the troublesome issues employees face most often."[9] At Barnett Banks when any computer terminal is on but idle, rather than a random screen design, each of Barnett's five beliefs with an appropriate picture accompanying it scrolls continuously.

When these approaches to communication are effectively applied, there is clear evidence of the relationship between that communication and on-the-job application. Our survey respondents were asked two questions:

"To what extent does management actively communicate the basic beliefs described in the attached statement?"

"To what extent do you feel basic beliefs are used to guide day-to-day decisions and activities in your company?"

The choice of answers to each question was:

Not at All	Limited Extent	Moderate Extent	Considerable Extent	Great Extent
1	2	3	4	5

In the following three tables, the scores shown are the average for the position indicated.

At The J. M. Smucker Company, where basic beliefs have been in practice since its founding, the answers on communication and application were very positive and consistent. There was minimal drop-off at positions down through the organization. Effective communication down the line creates the opportunity for application throughout the organization.

POSITION	COMMUNICATION SCORE	APPLICATION SCORE
Senior Management	4.0	5.0
Mid-Level Management	4.3	4.2
First Level Supervision	4.2	4.0
Nonmanagement	3.8	3.8

At Harley-Davidson, Inc., which has continued a remarkable turnaround under CEO Rich Teerlink, working the basic beliefs process is rather new. Results on the relationship between communication and application are mainly consistent with each other, but there is some drop-off as one moves down through the organization. Effective application can only follow effective communication.

POSITION	COMMUNICATION SCORE	APPLICATION SCORE
Board, Senior Management	4.4	4.1
Mid-Level Management/First Level Supervision	3.8	3.2
Nonmanagement/Hourly	2.8	2.8

As mentioned previously, AAA did a thorough job of involving its Clubs and National Office in seeking and stating basic beliefs. Somehow, when it came to communication, that involvement and excitement did not filter down through the National Office. They did not get the message at either management or nonmanagement levels. However, at Club level they got it!

AREA	COMMUNICATION SCORE	APPLICATION SCORE
National Office		
Management	2.2	2.4
Nonmanagement	2.6	2.4
Club Level		
CEO Small Club	3.7	3.8
CEO Medium Club	3.5	3.8
CEO Large Club	3.5	4.1
Club Management (Non-CEO)	3.6	3.6
Club Nonmanagement	3.4	3.5

Surveys provide a good way to bring these kinds of disparities among units to the surface so they can be addressed. In later chapters what these companies are doing to improve communication and all parts of their basic beliefs process will be discussed.

For all four companies, 500 participants answered this essay question:

"How would you suggest the basic beliefs be improved as far as how they are communicated?"

Those responses were categorized as follows:

CATEGORY	PERCENT
No change needed	13
Not sufficiently communicated	12
More emphasis in existing systems, publications	10
More emphasis on employee responsibility	9
More top management communication	9
More mid-management communication	7
Display framed beliefs throughout organization	6
Use actual examples with impact on results and communications	6
Build into all training/orientation programs	5
Build into all meetings, standing committees, etc.	4
All other responses	19

These results suggest that communication of beliefs is unending and that there are many ways to improve how it is accomplished. These specific responses provide additional ideas.

• Create opportunities for sharing ... where enhancing beliefs or deviating from them resulted in success or failure in certain endeavors ... at regional conferences, business line workshops, national publications, etc.

• ... [B]asic beliefs should be linked to business strategy. The beliefs should be guidelines to any decision which supports this business strategy.

- Not by hanging a plaque on the wall. Maybe by holding department meetings monthly or quarterly with all employees to determine if the department is carrying out the basic beliefs and how operations could be improved.

- I suggest that a video be produced (with examples) to show all employees the true meaning and purpose of the company beliefs. This presentation should become part of the orientation program. Also, the beliefs should be summarized on a small card for employees to carry on their person or keep at their work station.

- Should appear regularly in the newsletter around the plant.

- Continue the cascading education—ask that each group come away from the training with a set of goals or a "contract" on observable behaviors that support the beliefs.

- It is not communicated enough. People should be reminded on exactly how it works and who it all effects. People need to hear how important their role is.

- Current communication is efficient for those who receive it. The communication and training should be expanded to all employees.

- Possibly start all training sessions with the background and substance of the basic beliefs.

- These beliefs need to be reiterated more often to line and warehouse personnel because churn and job tedium make these beliefs relatively unimportant.

- Focus on a particular belief each week or month and initiate contests, programs, games to correspond with and emphasize the message of that belief.

- Rather than post it on the wall it should be actively used as a yardstick in measuring daily decisions. Management should actively lead discussions and reviews of actions based on the beliefs.

- A lot of employees do not know the beliefs behind the company—what do they really mean? How does it affect everyone—not just the branch employee who sees outside customers all the time?

To sum it all up, effective communication of beliefs must be:

Participative: Telling alone does not produce sufficient buy-in.

Relevant: Understanding how beliefs "fit" and apply on the job.

Credible: Involving all managers directly in communicating beliefs and then acting on them.

Motivational: Reinforcing the positive benefits of sound beliefs on the company and all stakeholders.

You can find and state basic beliefs and they can be effectively communicated, but nothing of substance happens unless they are applied—so let's get to the action.

Basic Beliefs Process	
1. Determine	4. APPLY
2. Articulate	5. Reward
3. Communicate	6. Review

C H A P T E R

F I V E

MAKING SURE IT ALL WORKS

People get paid for producing desirable results at whatever level or job. They don't get paid for knowing and being able to recite the company's basic beliefs. So what's the connection? Get those beliefs off the wall plaques and into the heads and hearts of all employees.

As we all realize, even when beliefs are stated and communicated they can break down at the application level. Thomas A. Stewart wrote in *Fortune*: "Several years ago I happened upon an employee attitude survey taken at a Fortune 500 industrial. Part of it asked workers about the company's statement of values—a fairly typical list of six, articulated a year or so previously, that included quality, integrity, respect for individuals, and profitability. The survey asked employees whether they had heard about each of the values and if they believed that the company meant and did what it said—if it walked the talk. Nearly all the employees were aware of the company's values statement, but only 60% believed the company actually meant it. Surprised by the low numbers, I described the survey to a consultant who specialized in employee-attitude surveys. What he said shocked me: 'Those are really high scores.'"[1]

I know Prudential has beliefs. I have seen them etched in the lobby wall. But in some areas they just can't seem to get them off the wall and into the work and supervision. First were the shenanigans and beliefs breakdowns in selling fraudulent limited partnerships. Now comes life insurance—misrepresentation, forgery, adding to premiums on existing policies without the consent or knowledge of the client. A $35 million record fine. Customer reimbursements could cost hundreds of millions more. These were not just a few isolated "rogues." It was widespread. Nearly 1,000 employees have been fired. Chairman Ryan said, "The improper practices cited by the task force are intolerable to Prudential."[2] It seems a little late to find a situation of this scope "intolerable." So, how do we do it right?

One good approach is to smoke out potential rogues before you get them. Hiring people who share your beliefs in the first place is not a bad initial step to help insure commitment and application: "Creating the right environment is a symphonic process, involving such disciplines as selection, appraisal, job assignment and mentoring. Step one is hiring the right people. Asks [consultant] Jim Collins rhetorically: 'How do you get people to share your values? You don't. You find people who share them and eject those who don't.'"[3]

The intent of each belief must be written into strategy statements, policies, plans, systems and procedures, job descriptions and performance review forms, raw material and product standards, personnel manuals, and the like. Staff groups are key facilitators. Basic beliefs officers or committees can orchestrate the effort. When preparing this transition to application, recognize that some beliefs may need more or less emphasis at different levels or functions. A merit belief like "Remain an independent company" needs emphasis at board and CEO level. An ethic belief about honesty or equality applies to every level, function, work group, and job across the company. A merit belief like "Technological leader in our industry" needs primary emphasis where that can be influenced. All of this translates the general intent of any belief into more specific guidelines for decision making and action.

For example, American Commercial Lines (ACL), a division of CSX, sees customer service as a critical belief. That belief is translated specifically into appropriate policies and procedures: "American Commercial Lines is committed to providing outstanding quality transportation and communication services that consistently satisfy our customers' expectations in a manner that makes it easy to do business with the company. ACL will meet this commitment by:

- Implementing measurements and programs that focus upon the service needs and expectation of customers.
- Establishing and maintaining policies and procedures designed to consistently improve service in a cost-effective manner.
- Developing information and communication systems created to efficiently support ACL sales and service efforts in a timely and responsive manner.

Above all else, ACL seeks to extend its service leadership through highly professional people dedicated to the standard of superior service. This will differentiate the Company from its competitors and maintain ACL as the carrier of choice."[4]

This is an example of how to build the intent of a people belief into policies, procedures, and practices. Ginsburg and Miller tell how one of their clients increased applications relating to a belief about employee safety:

"1. Post company-wide safety performance in visible locations;

2. Introduce a safety incentive program;

3. Increase safety emphasis in new employee orientation. Educate, monitor, and appraise supervisors on safety;

4. Review safety performance by senior staff more frequently;

5. Charge accident costs back to divisions;

6. Implement lost time return program;

7. Give Safety Committee more authority as 'watch dog';

8. Appoint and train first-aid staff for each location."

To ensure that strategies become actions, accountability and dates for completion were assigned. More important, however, job descriptions for each manager, supervisor, and crew leader were rewritten to include employee safety. Departmental objectives and individual performance expectations ensured their attention at every organizational level."[5]

Through its policies, procedures, and practices the organization must make known the specific meaning and standards it has for its beliefs. Mary Rabaut of Gemini Consulting well illustrates this point: "Live 'em. That's the hardest part. Says Mary Rabaut: 'Putting your values into words isn't enough. The company's policies have to be consistent with them.' Andrall Pearson, a former president of PepsiCo now teaching at Harvard business school, calls the void between the real and the ideal a values gap and says it is 'the largest single source of cynicism and skepticism in the workplace today.' Example: the plaque on the wall says, PEOPLE ARE OUR MOST PRECIOUS ASSET, but the company has just laid off thousands. THE ACME SUITCASE—FINEST IN THE WORLD, says the plaque; on the production line, every tenth handle is being sewn on upside down."[6]

To close that "values gap" all employees need to understand how beliefs apply specifically to their jobs. They must be carried through policies and procedures, and built into decisions, practices, and behavior. A large part of management and supervision is facilitating that transition. "Talking and walking" the beliefs is essential. The benefits to any employee for consistent application must be reinforced. Those benefits include:

- Satisfaction of doing it right the first time.
- Pride in being a part of a company that really cares.
- Positive feelings from performance of work team members.
- Recognition and reward for outstanding application.
- Knowledge that beliefs influence sustained company success and growth and that translates into better job security and potential.

Beliefs-based behavior, performance, and relationships become the way work is done and contribute to positive results. The more positive the results, the greater the motivation to apply beliefs.

To illustrate this last point we asked our survey respondents this question:

"Please describe an important decision where you felt the outcome was positive because it was strongly influenced by the basic beliefs."

When all responses were categorized, 49 percent concerned decisions about products or customers, 27 percent about human resources, and 24 percent all others. The following specific responses are typical of those reported.

The American Automobile Association

- A teaming process is currently being carried out in Travel Information/Publishing Operations. Employees to a greater extent are becoming empowered. Communication has become better from employee to employee and management to employee and all across the matrix. The work environment has improved.

- As a direct result of the Club's active political support of a statewide reform measure which was clearly in the best interests of members and other motorists, reform was enacted, even though it cost the Club approximately $400,000 per year in lost drivers' license and license plate renewal fees.

- We decided to integrate our Auto Travel and Travel Agency departments. The process involved considerable change on the part of many people. However, we now have far better qualified counselors who can respond to our customers' total needs.

- The decision to educate employees for the reason of having the best educated employees to serve our members. What we have seen is little turnover in employees and much repeat business.

- Members were given discounts and other additional benefits to help offset the sting of a dues increase. Staff was empowered to waive dues increases when they thought it would save the membership. This proactive approach to handling a difficult but necessary decision has led to a positive renewal rate and limited member reaction.

The J. M. Smucker Company

- Issues associated with ingredient label statements were decided based on ethical considerations rather than economic issues. Key to doing the right thing.

- The company promoted from within the first female plant manager in Memphis, Tennessee. This was implemented due to the company promoting and enforcing its basic belief in its people/employees.

- Discharge of employee for sexual harassment done with discretion, maintaining the privacy of all concerned to the greatest extent possible.

- Independence—Smucker's issue of a Class B Common Stock strongly reinforced the desire to remain independent in that it allowed greater institutional investment in the company while not providing any voting rights to holders of Class B stock.

- I remember a specific time that our community's football team was going to the state finals. Many of the union employees wanted to be able to go to the game. The company rescheduled the production runs to be able to produce what was needed with the least amount of employees, excusing those who wanted to go support our football team. We lost the game, but the example of basic beliefs was seen as positive when the company was sensitive to the requests of the employees.

Harley-Davidson, Inc.

- The decision to change post-retirement health benefits and what those benefits would be was strongly influenced by the business process (basic beliefs).

- Many times grievances and adversarial bargaining were avoided by living the values.

- The 'reorganization' of the marketing research work unit under the leadership of the director of business planning. All the elements of the business process (basic beliefs) were taken into consideration and resulted in a team which is productive, focused on value-added activities and 'happy' in the process.

- There is a process redesign for Order Management/Sales Promotion. Part of this has been an extra effort to live by the Business Process.

Barnett Banks, Inc.

- I am very proud of the role Barnett plays in various charitable organizations. We do make a positive difference in our community.

- An employee was persistent on finding a lost check even after all trails led to a dead end. She eventually pursued the vault until they found work in a tray under a desk which had not been processed.

- A very old customer's cable TV was shut off because they said they did not receive payment. I ordered canceled checks and called the cable company to help straighten it out. The cable company was impressed and the customer was relieved.

All of the above responses were indicative of how beliefs influence long-term success from an operational or day-to-day perspective. We also wanted to see how our respondents felt beliefs influenced the development of effective strategies. We asked them these questions:

"To what extent are basic beliefs used in the development of your company's future strategy?"

"To what extent should basic beliefs be used in developing your company's future strategy?"

Again, the response scale was:

Not at All	Limited Extent	Moderate Extent	Considerable Extent	Great Extent
1	2	3	4	5

The average response to the "How are they used?" was 3.9 with a range from 3.6 to 4.4. The average response to "How should they be used?" was 4.5 with a range from 4.4 to 4.9. That's respectable, but leaves room for improvement. The following selected quotes show how people down through each organization feel their company *is using* beliefs to set strategy.

The American Automobile Association

- Balancing our responsibility to be financially successful while providing world-class service to our members, we ask ourselves: 1) Is this new service/product able to generate revenue? 2) Is this in the best interest of our members (short- and long- range)? 3) Have we asked our members how they feel about it? 4) Will our employees feel positive about their role in implementing it? 5) Does this enhance the value of AAA membership?

- There has been a recent effort to more specifically include consideration of basic beliefs in the formulation of strategies as well as other policy. This is in large part due to an increased awareness and a heightened importance of the basic beliefs promulgated by the (new) CEO.

The J. M. Smucker Company

- *Growth and people*—The company tries to promote from within the organization whenever possible to develop its employees. *Ethics*—Ethics training is offered to assist an employee in making the right decision in the workplace. *Independence*—In order to maintain its independence, the company continuously looks for acquisitions to increase its net worth to further minimize a 'corporate takeover.' *Quality*—We continue to stress in advertising that Smucker was founded on quality.

- Emphasis on products that improve quality of life, emphasis on products helping company to grow, emphasis on products of best quality—avoidance of misleading labeling or use of juice concentrates in lieu of fruit content, despite its use by competitors to our detriment.

Harley-Davidson, Inc.

- The board spends considerable time reviewing, assessing, and evolving corporate strategy. In each situation we try to respect the values, vision, and stockholders' interests. There is excellent discipline.

- In trying to meet stockholders' interests, the company is trying to invest in future capacity yet maintain quality and improve productivity which will all impact cash flow.

Barnett Banks, Inc. (Did not complete this question.)

We asked for comments on "how basic beliefs *should* be used in setting future strategy." They are included to show there is concern in the organizations that beliefs be fully considered in strategic decision making. These were selected because they reasonably reflect general thoughts across the companies and apply to any organization trying to build beliefs into its strategic deliberations.

- This is difficult in that our division has not put together a full strategic plan for two years. In the past, most plans have not addressed suppliers, employees, or society.

- Basic beliefs are the touchstone in developing overall future strategy. The failure, where existent, comes in applying the strategy developed. 'What is best for the customer' is often subordinated to actions increasing the P&L bottom line.

- Sometimes I believe corporate decisions are internally (headquarters) driven. Affiliates in the field should be asked to provide more input to corporate decision making. Without this, it can become a 'we and they.'

- Sometimes I have the feeling that plans for the company's future center around what will make money. I realize we must have money to provide and expand services. However, I feel if the process took into consideration the future of customer needs as related to technology we would seldom move in directions that would cause misuse of funds or energy.

- Our beliefs are still very important to the company as a whole. But sometimes I worry that they are being compromised more and more as we grow.

Belief-based actions, multiplied by the hundreds across the corporation every day, will have an unseen but major influence on the company results. Beliefs become the template through which every decision must pass. They benefit every stakeholder. The customer receives a quality product at a fair price. The investor receives real value over time. The employee shares in the pride and stability of an organization that practices what it preaches.

Gaining application of beliefs is not easy. It takes special effort in situations that involve a lot of independence in the relationship between employee and customer. Brokers, tellers, salespersons, professionals, and consultants are often on their own as they apply the company beliefs to decisions and relationships with those they serve. Beliefs about honesty, trust, and service must be very thoroughly built into their training and on-the-job mentoring. Performance requirements must take beliefs into account to see that short-term actions don't inhibit longer-term success. Monitoring practices through performance controls, customer feedback, and spot audits must be used and publicized.

Similar thinking must be given to supervisory levels. Sumitomo, Daiwa, and Kidder, as described earlier, got into millions and billions of dollars of trouble before anyone noticed. Did no one think the increasing size of those dealings might mean something was awry? What was going on was not totally concealed. Management was so far removed from what was going on they either didn't know or knew and condoned it. If these "big rogues" did all this damage, how many "little rogues" are each doing a bit of damage each day? This is not to say that effective beliefs application will totally prevent this from happening. Supervisory training in how to manage beliefs application and act through beliefs will help reduce this damage.

Much needs to be done to assure application when a company dramatically changes the historic sense of a belief about people and how work is accomplished. Texas Instruments provides an example. There had been a "do your job and don't say anything" approach with an autocratic, top-down management style. That was changed to self-managed work teams with supervisors as facilitators. A tough task! "Change has not come easily or quickly, however. Even in the best cases, it takes about two years for a TI work team to take on its own day-to-day management, as the work process usually has to be completely redesigned. Supervisors have to recast themselves as facilitators—or be replaced. Information systems have to be changed to give the team members access to product cost data. And there's the up-front financial cost: TI boosted U.S. training spending 17% last year [1992], to $35 million."[7] Be firm and thorough, but have patience when changing the intent of a basic belief.

The change at Texas Instruments was a 180-degree turn in how a basic belief was applied. To gain the new behaviors desired for such a change, every aspect of the performance system surrounding the environment where the behavior takes place must be reviewed:

- structure, job descriptions, work rules
- work unit or team size, selection, leadership
- information requirements and controls
- recognition, pay, and reward systems
- management and supervisory responsibility
- training
- support systems and procedures
- work layout, tools, equipment

If the performance system supports the old or current behavior, there are too many consequences to expect much change. People are comfortable where they are. They will tend to resist change unless every facet of the performance system is brought into sync with the change in the intent of how a belief is applied. When that is done, the desired behavior change can take place.

Management at every level has to lead the beliefs application charge. They must know what is going on with basic beliefs and decision making and action. Leaders who follow beliefs will have followers who lead beliefs. Robert Haas of Levi Strauss says it well: "How does a CEO manage for values? The first responsibility for me and for my team is to examine critically our own behaviors and management styles in relation to the behaviors and values that we profess and to work to become more consistent with the values that we are articulating. It's tough work. We all fall off the wagon. But you can't be one thing and say another. People have unerring detection systems for fakes, and they won't put up with them. They won't put values into practice if you're not."[8]

Every employee, not just management, must walk the beliefs talk. Each one must know it is a part of his or her responsibility to raise questions and offer input about beliefs when involved in or affected by any strategic or operational decision.

Application of beliefs is enhanced when recognition is given. That is the subject of the next chapter.

RECOGNITION—KEY TO MOTIVATION

When outstanding results are accomplished from the application of beliefs, continued motivation is enhanced through recognition and reward. The words "outstanding" or "excellent" or "beyond the call of duty" are important. All employees throughout the organization must know that the consistent application of beliefs to day-by-day decisions and activities is the standard. At Ford, "Quality Is Job One"—and that's expected. General benefits to all employees for the application of beliefs must be constantly reinforced through all mediums. Revenue growth, customer loyalty, and consistent product quality are the keys to any organization's long-term growth and reputation. They lead to a real sense of security and even employment gains. That's a good message. However, specific recognition and reward for outstanding application should motivate all to realize the significance of beliefs.

Both financial reward and nonfinancial recognition are important. K-T provides a program that covers both. Any employee in the company can complete a form describing an associate's outstanding support and application of basic beliefs. Once each quarter a committee composed of a cross section of employees reviews the submissions and selects and recognizes the most qualified employee. Once each year the committee selects the most outstanding of the quarterly recipients. Financial reward and nonfinancial recognition through the company newsletter are given to the quarterly and annual winners. The employee who receives the annual award, along with spouse or friend, is given an all-expense paid trip to any place in the world where K-T has an office. I know the power of that program to create pride and generate support of the application of K-T's basic beliefs day-by-day and at all levels.

"A recent *New York Times* article ... stresses the importance of tying rewards to values. In the 1960s, pay was tied to profit; in the 1980s pay was tied to performance. We feel strongly that the 1990s will find more companies reexamining the strategic implications of their compensation practices and specifically looking at the extent to which they reinforce corporate values."

The article continues: "Reuben Mark, CEO of Colgate-Palmolive, states that 'putting money on the line puts teeth into management's value statements.' Constantine Nicandros, CEO of Conoco, Inc., made environmental criteria a component of the incentive program because he feels 'money is a good way to let people know the company values certain types of behavior.' Chemical Bank rewards customer satisfaction. Several of our clients have begun to reward the values of teamwork, innovation, and safety, in addition to growth and profitability.

"Non-financial rewards, such as recognition programs, leaves of absence, time off, and merchandise incentives, have also proven productive. Peer pressure, involvement, and pride have been shown to be as influential as money in gaining commitment. Combined with training, the dual powers of financial reinforcement and personal recognition are extremely potent motivational forces."[1]

We asked our company respondents this question:

"How are behavior and actions that support basic beliefs recognized and rewarded? Circle those that apply."

The categories shown were included with the question, to be circled as appropriate.

CATEGORY	PERCENT TOTAL RESPONSE
A. Specific one-time cash bonus	7.9
B. Considered in year-end bonus	4.8
C. Considered in wage and salary increases	12.3
D. Considered in job promotion	10.9
E. Individual recognition by supervisor	19.5
F. Special noncash award	21.5
G. Recognition in company publications	13.0
H. Other	3.6
I. They are not	6.5

While many different forms of financial and nonfinancial recognition were included in these responses, it is interesting that the nonfinancial response was greater.

Our respondents answered this essay question:

"How would you suggest ___(company name)___ basic beliefs be improved as far as how application is reinforced and rewarded?"

These specific quotes provide many ideas as to how these employees felt beliefs should be applied, measured, and rewarded. I have commented on each one in parentheses.

Barnett Banks, Inc.

- Through customer surveys give recognition at the branch or department level rather than just individually. (*Consider both team and individual recognition and rewards.*)
- Projects should not be rewarded for speed of implementation but rather quality and speed. I've often seen speed as the driving factor and then saw people wondering why they had problems. (*Rewards for application of beliefs must be for the right reasons.*)
- Why should we have to reward? This is what a Barnett team member should do all the time. (*Yes, but consider truly exceptional applications.*)

- Many of my peers live by the philosophy of our beliefs and vision statement every day but since they don't toot their own horns, no one will ever know the impact they have on our customers and our community. (*Need to find ways to recognize these applications.*)

The American Automobile Association

- Establish a blue-ribbon panel of members, employees of Clubs and the national office, CEOs, board and senior national office staff to judge quarterly submissions of experiences across the Association in each belief category. Establish a total commitment reward—also annual winners. Panel to establish some criteria for winning. All submissions receive recognition among Association constituency. (*A very specific idea. Ambitious, but lots of appeal.*)
- Reward system contradicts basic beliefs. On members, for example, Clubs receive national recognition for growth. If you invest in systems, technology, or the future at the short-term expense of growth, you run the risk of being a failure under current reward systems. (*Rewards must balance short- and long-term applications.*)
- A direct correlation between adhering to the beliefs and performance evaluation/reward should be drawn. However, we should not necessarily reward behavior that should be expected within the culture but rather outstanding examples of such and creative application of them. (*Building outstanding application into performance rewards will make it stick.*)
- Finding an approved way to measure service excellence and offer tangible rewards for top-flight customer service. (*Must be measured to give appropriate rewards.*)

Harley-Davidson, Inc.

- Recognition of departments, individuals, teams that practice the values through company publications, division meetings, etc. H-D merchandise or dinner certificates for folks would be appropriate. Don't create a formal program, but allow spontaneous recognition by supervisors, senior management, peers, etc. (*Making part of recognition spontaneous keeps it fresh and exciting, but it is also easier to overlook.*)

- Peer evaluations on how people successfully comply with the Business Process (beliefs). (*Peer evaluation keeps belief recognition and reward honest and fair.*)

- Begin to promote and publicize those who use the values and get results. Demote or move those who get results in less healthy ways. Show by actions—public actions—that the organization can understand. (*Positive reinforcement is a powerful motivator, but appropriate penalties for major failures to apply beliefs make the positive even stronger.*)

The J. M. Smucker Company

- One way would be to include a special area on the employee's annual performance report. Here specific instances of applying the Basic Beliefs could be identified. (*Building beliefs into this form keeps them visible and stresses importance in a very positive, personal way.*)

- More positive reinforcement should be given by direct supervisors when a "right decision" or "action" is implemented by an employee due to that person considering the company's basic beliefs. (*There is no substitute for recognition from immediate supervisor.*)

- In our plant, employees really care about their peers and company. I would like to see a program where appreciation can be shared, i.e., Bulletin Boards. (*Nonfinancial recognition counts a lot.*)

- Singling out individuals or "teams" for behavior that supports the basic beliefs must be done carefully, because our company beliefs are themselves founded on moral and decent standards which all JMS employees *should* normally adhere to—without reward. However, in a society that is leaning towards selfishness and amoral standards, to acknowledge individuals or "teams" that illustrate our basic beliefs in practice/application would be beneficial. (*Excellent point—focus on "outstanding" application.*)

Bob Haas at Levi describes beliefs recognition and rewards this way: "One-third of a manager's raise, bonus, and other financial rewards depends on his or her ability to manage aspirationally [through beliefs]—the 'how' of management rather than the 'what.' That goes for decisions about succession planning as well.

"In some areas of the company, they're weighting it even more strongly. The point is, it's big enough to get people's attention. It's real. There's money attached to it. Giving people tough feedback and a low rating on aspirational management means improvement is necessary no matter how many pants they got out the door. Promotion is not in the future unless you improve.

"It's [pay] an influence but not the most important one. The key factors determining whether the values take or not will be individual commitment and desire and the peer pressure in the environment that we create. To me, the idea of a person as a marionette whose arms and legs start moving whenever you pull the pay string is too simplistic a notion of what motivates people in organizations."[2]

As Chase Manhattan Corp. fought its way back from late eighties' woes, CEO Labrecque put values back in place and put rewards in to make them work: "Even employees' performance evaluations are changing to include measures of their adherence to the new values. Soon, credit-card-division workers' pay may swing up or down by as much as 25% based on how they measure. Executives have already felt the effects of VisionQuest [a program from ARC International which includes determining beliefs] in their paychecks. Robert D. Hunter, executive vice president in charge of national consumer products, says less than half his compensation is tied to the performance of his own businesses, and 'it's amazing how that changes your attitude.'"[3]

Manugistics, Inc. does it this way: "The Elements of Excellence [basic beliefs] were introduced to the workforce at a kickoff event in which each of the employees received a plaque on which the Elements were etched. To ensure they weren't just plaques and platitudes, the company created the Individual and Team Excellence awards to reinforce the philosophies. The awards, which included plaques and cash, and are presented quarterly at company-wide employee meetings, publicly recognize those employees whose performance in meeting their business objectives clearly embodies the Elements of Excellence. 'We wanted to recognize people who are leading their business lives according to our ideals,' William Kaluza, CFO, of Manugistics explains."[4]

There is no limit to the ways belief-driven performance can be recognized and rewarded. "Something as simple as an award can help make a culture more innovative. In Japan, Sharp rewards top performers by putting them on a 'gold badge' project team that reports directly to the company president. The privilege instills pride and gets other employees scrambling for new ideas and products in the hope that they too may make the team.

"Awards can also encourage risk taking. About a year ago, the people in Du Pont's relocation department—who help move executives to new cities—thought they could boost productivity by installing a new computer system. The experiment failed but rather than chastise those who suggested it, the company in November presented them with a plaque that told them: We're proud of your effort and hope you try again as hard in years to come."[5]

We asked our respondents this question:

"Regardless of level to what extent do successful people in the company more frequently follow and apply the basic beliefs than less successful people?"

Not at All	Limited Extent	Moderate Extent	Considerable Extent	Great Extent
1	2	3	4	5

The average score was 3.6. The spread was 3.2 to 4.0. While not a bad response, one would like to see those numbers closer to 5. For all four companies the scores from senior management were higher than the scores from nonmanagement personnel. If it is not a self-serving response, that is a positive sign. One would hope that every CEO would answer with a "5."

Promotion is a very positive and visible way to reward those who make the organization's beliefs their work life: "Managers must be sure that what they actually do fosters rather than impedes ethical conduct. One sure way to send the word is by rewarding admirable behavior. No code of ethics and no amount of cajolery by the chief executive will have much effect if promotions regularly go to the people who pile up big numbers by cutting corners. Says [Stanford professor] Kirk Hanson: 'Senior management has got to find a way to create heroes, people who serve the company's competitive values—and also its social and ethical values.'"[6]

Positive reinforcement brings pride and recognition into accomplishment. It is a most powerful motivator to encourage those behaviors to continue. On the other side of the coin, basic beliefs violations cannot be ignored.

A psychologist friend of mine once said to me, "Yes means a lot more when you understand no." This principle applies to assessing the application of basic beliefs. Discipline or penalty practices should be in place to discourage failure to apply beliefs. These should be known throughout the organization. Penalties must be realistic and geared to the scope of the belief breakdown. Personal criticism should always be handled privately. Penalties should be made known for breakdowns that are public knowledge.

When breakdowns are properly disciplined, the grapevine rapidly spreads the reality of the organization's beliefs. One must be just as diligent in ferreting out and handling belief breakdowns as one is in recognizing and rewarding outstanding application. "An organization must provide both rewards for compliance to guidelines and sanctions when unethical actions are discovered. When unethical actions are not dealt with, word spreads that the organization is not really interested in ethics. In some cases a demotion, rather than firing, may be sufficient to make this point."[7]

Sometimes demotion is not enough: "Graydon Wood, Nynex's newly appointed ethics officer, says the job requires a realistic view of human behavior. Says he: 'You have to recognize that even with all the best programs, some employees do go wrong. Last year some marketing people didn't report properly, resulting in unjustified commissions. We fired them.'"[8]

SUMMARY

Following are results from our survey as to both belief reward and penalty. These questions were asked:

"To what extent are behavior and actions that support basic beliefs recognized and rewarded?"

"To what extent are behavior and actions that conflict with basic beliefs discouraged or disciplined?"

The choices for each question were:

Not at All	Limited Extent	Moderate Extent	Considerable Extent	Great Extent
1	2	3	4	5

Scores for all four companies on reward for application averaged 3.0 with a spread among the four from 2.8 to 3.2. Scores for all four companies on discipline for lack of application averaged 2.9 with a spread among the four from 2.7 to 3.2. With the effort each of these companies has invested in the belief process, I was surprised that both rewards and penalties were felt at only moderate levels. If ongoing application of beliefs is motivated by recognition for success and penalties for failure, then any company should gain significantly by improving practices in this area.

This comment from *Harvard Business Review* editor Rosabeth Kanter well summarizes this chapter on recognition for outstanding beliefs application and penalties for major breakdowns: "To be meaningful, values must enter into the daily life

of the organization, with violators punished and exemplars rewarded. Soon, the organization will equate abstract statements
of principle with concrete models and lessons. But the values
must reflect enduring commitments, not ephemeral notions.
Thus leaders who are tempted to manage through values had
better be prepared to examine their own—and to put their actions where their hearts are."[9]

The final part of the basic beliefs process is review: How are
we doing and are we up to date on our beliefs?

Basic Beliefs Process	
1. Determine	4. Apply
2. Articulate	5. Reward
3. Communicate	6. REVIEW

C H A P T E R

S E V E N

KEEP IMPROVING AND STAY IN TUNE WITH THE TIMES

The review step in the basic beliefs process has two parts: Monitoring to assess progress and pinpoint deviations and updating to see that beliefs and their intent are kept current with environmental change.

MONITORING PROGRESS

Assessing the effectiveness of a basic beliefs process requires a monitoring program. Developing such a program and seeing that it is implemented is an excellent responsibility for a basic beliefs officer or committee. A corollary responsibility is to see that the results of monitoring are consolidated and reported and needed action plans developed. General positive progress should be reported across the company. Any emerging problems should be brought to those responsible for analysis and resolution.

Monitoring occurs at all levels in the organization. The board of directors keeps watch on the CEO and executives to see that strategic conclusions and major operating plans to accomplish them are based on and support beliefs. Previously cited examples like ADM and Bausch & Lomb indicated that this monitoring needs improvement. Fortunately the impact of outside directors is on the increase: "Inside directors' influence on corporate boards has been eroding steadily over the past two decades. Boards are under greater pressure from shareholders to be independent from company management, keeping a strict and impartial eye over operations."[1]

For example, to clean up the top-level beliefs problem at Archer Daniels Midland Company, a board committee produced a governance report. "Among the main recommendations in the report: The board should be cut to as few as nine members, the majority being outsiders; [m]anagement should be limited to three seats, down from five; [c]ommittees should be entirely composed of outsiders, except for the executive committee; [o]utside directors should step down at age 70.... If the board actually puts into practice what it has approved on paper, ADM could catapult from a company regularly shellacked by investor activists to one of exemplary corporate openness."[2]

Down through the organization various monitoring approaches and programs should be in place to help managers, supervisors, and team leaders check the effectiveness of the beliefs process. Of course, the best way is to be out on the floor with eyes and ears open. When Ford bought Jaguar it went through awful times: falling sales and profits; shedding 33 percent of staff; harder work for all; dealer mistrust. Dale Gambill, vice president of customer care, gathered Jaguar managers together to talk about the customer. He got a different response: "As soon as I started in on customer care, these people said, 'Hey, let's forget the customer for a minute here. You aren't taking care of us,' Gambill says. 'I hadn't realized how much pent-up frustration there was. These people spent two days venting. They said we had no clear vision for the future. They said we had too many competing sets of values among the departments. They said we never learned anything from our mistakes and were just constantly going around putting out fires. And they told me we had to start getting more customer-focused.'"[3]

The standard performance reports should be reviewed for progress or problems that seem to be beliefs based. Any recommendation, suggestion, or new approach should be questioned and assessed to see that appropriate beliefs are considered.

Other indirect and more spontaneous approaches to monitoring can also be worthwhile:

- Focus group or informal work unit sessions to discuss how the beliefs are working and how the process could be improved.
- Core sampling of customers, suppliers, investors, and the community to see how they feel about beliefs.
- Include questions concerning basic beliefs in employee attitude surveys.
- Random or spur of the moment checkpoints with a focus on beliefs:

  —Talk with a top-level customer.

  —Join a sales or service person on a call.

  —Talk with a new employee on orientation and beliefs.

  —Visit a new acquisition.

  —Drop in on a product design or safety committee meeting.

  —Visit a subsidiary to sit in on a decision-making or planning meeting.

  —Check on a "hotline" problem to see if it is addressed.

  —Sit in on a training program.

To monitor the effectiveness of beliefs application, appropriate measures must be identified or developed. For example, Ginsburg and Miller report the key values described by one firm:

"VALUE	MEASURED BY
Profitability	Return on invested assets
Integrity	Reputation; customer and community feedback
Quality	Product standards and quality control measurements
People	Employee retention, development, and promotion
Safety	Days without time lost due to accidents
Productivity	Production tonnage rates per plant employee"[4]

Beliefs like honesty, fairness, and equality can be measured by surveying those affected by the belief. Using "360-degree" evaluations is a good internal way to see that these beliefs about fairness and the like are being applied at both management and nonmanagement levels. GE uses this approach: "The 360 process begins with HR devising a detailed questionnaire pegged to the behaviors the corporate culture values most. The questionnaire usually asks employees whether their manager 'keeps me informed,' 'does not interfere with my job,' and so forth. Everyone who works with the manager—boss, peers, and subordinates—contributes to the evaluation. At GE, which uses 360s for more senior people, the output is a bluntly worded report that the manager discusses behind closed doors with an HR pro and then with his boss. 'Development needs'—the euphemism for problems—get plenty of attention.

"A classic example of making the soft stuff hard, the 360-degree evaluation can provide great benefits. First, it provides a means of systematically making subjective yet apparently unbiased judgements about people.... Second, the 360 process is designed to force supervisors into the sort of candid, face-to-face discussions that most supervisors would prefer to avoid. Most important for leadership, feedback from 360s can signal opportunities to learn. Growth begins when individuals reach a more objective understanding of their strengths and weaknesses, enabling them to take responsibility for their own development."[5]

Peers and subordinates are the right people to involve in supervisory assessment. They bring reality to how beliefs like honesty and fairness are being applied and how that might be improved. Getting the right people involved in the beliefs monitoring process can be critical in another way. PaineWebber Group Inc. has hired Ted Levine as its top lawyer: "Mr. Levine is one of a new breed of lawyer signing up at Wall Street firms, as continuing scandals and regulatory crackdowns force the industry to recognize that it needs to police itself better. In the six months since his arrival in PaineWebber's executive offices, Mr. Levine already has implemented a series of measures designed to keep the big brokerage house—hit somewhat worse than competitors by recent customer lawsuits—out of further trouble.

"Among his biggest changes so far: establishing a dispute-resolution system to settle tough cases early, and placing the legal department in charge of the employee group that handles sales practice complaints. In the past, the complaint staff consulted with lawyers only on an ad-hoc basis. To make the new system work, Mr. Levine has sought, and received, authorization to add as many as 20 lawyers to his staff, which currently numbers about 40. He also is planning to establish a confidential hotline to the legal department for employees who seek to report suspicious activity.

"... The moves mark a bold departure from the traditional image of a brokerage firm's top legal officer as a mostly passive clerk. At worst, Wall Street's in-house lawyers have been water-carriers for management rather than defenders of their true client—the firms themselves."[6]

Establishing a hotline or other systems and approaches to report beliefs violations requires careful thought and ongoing attention. Just because such programs are established doesn't mean they will work. In an article in the latest *California Management Review*, Joseph Badaracco of Harvard Business School and Allen Webb of McKinsey, a consultancy, try to explain why firms are sometimes led astray. Rather than focusing on senior managers—who invariably determine a company's ethical stance—the researchers chose to interview young high-flyers about their ethical dilemmas. Half of the fledgling managers had worked at firms with formal ethics programmes; all had studied ethics as part of their MBAs.

"Their experience makes depressing reading. In many companies, 'behaving ethically' meant no more than performing well and being loyal to the company. As long as they did not break the law, young managers were generally encouraged not to 'over-invest' in ethical behavior; indeed, sleazy but successful managers seemed to be granted 'immunity' to ethical strictures. Less than a third of interviewees believed that their firms respected employees who blew the whistle on unethical practices. As a result, in only one company did a young manager consult his organization's ethical code when facing a crisis."[7]

No employees want to rat on their own team, coworkers, or friends. Yet if one buys into the company's beliefs and sees decisions or actions that ignore or violate them, that's also hard to live with. No one wants an "Orwellian" or "Gestapo-like" system, and yet avenues are needed for employees to feel secure in reporting beliefs malpractice. Sam Walton had an open door all the way down to entry level jobs, and people used it. He studied their concerns and took action if he agreed beliefs had been violated. He protected those who came. It worked because he made "people values" work, and everybody knew it.

Contrast that "open door" approach to the Allstate Insurance Company approach: "Myles Barchas had become one of Allstate's top-selling salesmen—the best in the 550-agent Dallas region—by his 29th birthday in 1993. Working 7-day weeks, he had amassed 3,200 customer accounts, nearly twice the company average. Allstate, headquartered in Northbrook, Illinois, showered Barchas with awards and honors and free exotic vacations that he never had time to accept.

"Then one day Barchas's world exploded. Deeply disturbed that his superiors were ordering agents to break state laws that protected consumers from discrimination, he began to blow the whistle. Though the company never admitted doing anything wrong, Barchas's evidence resulted in Allstate's paying what was then the largest insurance fine in Texas history. But Barchas paid too. He was stalked and chased by private eyes for periods spanning six months, according to internal company documents. And with the flick of a computer switch, Allstate took away his business."[8]

Behavior that drastically violates beliefs can occur in very sensitive situations with major potential risks for any who might report it. Perceived consequences may be so great that it won't be reported until much too late. The recent exposé of sexual harassment at Astra USA is a case in point: "What is especially disturbing about Astra is the way the alleged harassment emanated from the top—then coursed its way down through the organization. Legions of women who felt embarrassed and angry nonetheless conformed to an unacceptable standard of behavior set by the subsidiary's very own CEO. So, too, did their male colleagues, many of whom later said they also considered Astra's conduct offensive.

"As the Astra case suggests, few people have the fortitude or the financial wherewithal to blow the proverbial whistle. Some Astra employees were daunted by the prospect of taking on a deep-pocketed corporation—especially since those who did complain allege they were targeted for retaliation. Economic need meant others put up with behavior they felt was degrading. Many of those interviewed also said they feared complaints would only result in a reputation as a trouble maker—something that would haunt them in the job market. 'If another pharmaceutical company knows you're involved in something like that, your chances of being hired are slim,' says Mary Ann Lowe, a former rep who left in 1991. 'Plus, it's very personal. Nobody wants to go public with sexual harassment. You know that if it ever went to trial, you'd be on trial, not the harasser.' With the alleged harassment sanctioned at the top, many women who felt harassed—and the men who sympathized with them—simply quit."[9]

Finding answers to prevent or spot this kind of beliefs violation early takes sensitive thought. These suggestions may stimulate thinking. Hotline programs must reach high up in the corporation, beyond any department, division, or geographically distant subsidiary. Any such program must totally protect the security of those reporting until action steps may require identification. Throughout any such situation, senior management must take a beliefs approach that seeks accurate verification of the event, true cause, and just action. Off-site meetings, development programs, and company-sponsored social events should be randomly attended by those outside the group involved. Management at any level should get down one level often enough to have a reasonable idea of what's going on.

It is not sound practice to shoot the messenger: "There are another 21 suits by alleged whistle-blowers still in the works. Some of these could be potential land mines. In an arbitration case now before the National Association of Securities Dealers, two former Prudential Insurance managers charge they brought sales abuses to Ryan's [Chairman and CEO] attention but that their complaints were ignored, supporting documents destroyed, and that they were fired in retaliation. The company says the managers were dismissed for failure to supervise and says it expects to be fully vindicated."[10]

In these organizations it will take a long time and a lot of positive change in the basic beliefs process to gain back trust that management cares, that it makes a difference to apply beliefs and to report any beliefs violations.

There are many ways to open channels for employees to report beliefs violations: "In the last five years there has been a sizable increase in the number of firms with advisory councils, whistle blowers' hotlines, ombudspersons and ethics officers. These strategies indicate firms recognize that employees may face moral dilemmas, and suggest that management supports their efforts to make the right decisions. For instance, Motorola has a business Ethics Compliance Committee that is charged with interpreting, clarifying, communicating and adjudicating the company's code. Without a committee or ombudsperson assigned to that task, it would be difficult to understand how codes could be enforced adequately or how alleged code violations could be adjudicated effectively and fairly."[11]

Ethics (basic beliefs) officers are on the increase and they find the hotline a powerful beliefs monitoring tool: "More and more companies are appointing full-time ethics officers, generally on the corporate vice-presidential level, who report directly to the chairman or an ethics committee of top officers. One of the most effective tools these ethics specialists employ is a hotline through which workers on all levels can register complaints or ask about questionable behavior. At Raytheon Corp., Paul Pullen receives some 100 calls a month. Around 80% involve minor issues that he can resolve on the spot or refer to the human resources department. Another 10% of callers are simply looking for a bit of advice. But about ten times a month, a caller reports some serious ethical lapse that Pullen must address with senior management. Says he: 'Most people have high standards, and they want to work in an atmosphere that is ethical. The complaints come from all levels, and they are typical of what you would find in any business: possible conflicts of interest, cheating on time cards, cheating on expense reports.'"[12]

Our survey respondents supported the need to surface and correct actions based on beliefs violations. They were asked this question:

> "In your work and the work around you when there is conflict between what is actually happening and the intent of the basic beliefs, what do you do about it?"

The first answer to be checked was "Go along with the situation as it is," and that got 12.8 percent of the responses. The second answer was "Correct the situation or bring it to the attention of someone who can do something about it," and that got 87.2 percent of the responses. As we didn't ask, and hindsight says we should have, we don't know how many of the 87.2 percent came through the organizational structure and how many came through any hotline. But in either case, 87.2 percent is a good response. However, the range of answers to "Go along with it" among the four companies was 0 percent to 28 percent; and within one company, one unit responded 13 percent and another unit 41 percent. There is never an end to the beliefs work to be done and the monitoring needed to check it.

The scope of an effective monitoring program should provide answers to these questions:

1. Are the best measures for assessing progress on the basic beliefs process in place?
2. Is the intent of beliefs consistently built into policies, procedures, and practices?
3. How well are the beliefs applied to both strategic decisions and the day-to-day activities that support them?

4. How do employees, customers, investors, and communities feel about the company's basic beliefs and how those beliefs affect them?

5. Do leaders model and take accountability for managing the basic beliefs process in their areas of responsibility?

UPDATING INTENT

Every organization is faced with environmental change—technological breakthroughs, economic and demographic trends, new societal values, legislative requirements, and global competitive pressures. Given these dynamics, the intent or manifestation of beliefs needs review and update. The key is to take advantage of appropriate environmental change while insuring that the decisions and activities affected retain the intent of the beliefs.

As we move from a focus on individual job responsibilities to empowered team responsibilities, the current policies and practices by which we measure, recognize, reward, and manage employees must be changed without losing the intent of our beliefs about people. As public concern and legislation about the environment in which we operate increase, current policies and practices that support beliefs about the community and the environment must be modified while maintaining the intent of our beliefs.

Global competition introduces new challenges about how to apply long-standing beliefs. In some countries bribes are the way in; kickbacks are standard operating procedure; and child labor and copyright infringement are condoned. These practices must be dealt with while we keep intact the intent of our beliefs about honesty, integrity, and legality. The computer technology explosion has led to increasing concerns about any information being available to anyone. Practices must be governed by policies and procedures that protect our beliefs about individual privacy. Reengineering, downsizing, and outsourcing continue in many companies. Beliefs about the importance of people, long-term growth, fairness, and honesty must be integrated and applied to decisions about these activities. As the gap in income growth between lower and upper levels increases, compensation practices as they impact our beliefs about people, fairness, and empowerment need review.

Given a particular external or internal change, beliefs themselves may need to be broadened, narrowed, combined, or reworded. But their meaning and intent should not change. From its beginning K-T had a belief that read: "Stay with and build on our leadership in process facilitation." Over the years it has broadened. It now reads: "Enhance and leverage our superior reputation as we build upon our worldwide leadership in process facilitation supported by consulting and skill building." "Consulting and skill building" were added to assure continued leadership in process facilitation. This also helped broaden K-T's reputation from a "training organization" to a "consulting organization." These changes have not modified the original intent of this belief. First, it keeps limited creative resources focused on improving problem-solving and decision-making processes and developing new processes such as strategy formulation and project management. Second, it helps guard against our acquiring or developing more general consulting programs that would diffuse K-T's leadership position.

Updates should be periodic—once every year or two—or immediate, given the potential impact of a major change. Making sure that beliefs are updated is another function for the basic beliefs officer or committee, first to consolidate significant internal or external change from within or outside the company, second to determine what aspects of the operation would be affected by any such change and how the beliefs would be involved, and third to make sure that senior management reviews and approves those conclusions and that they are referred to those who should deal with them.

Richard L. Osborne provides a vivid example of what happens when this kind of review is not done. To paraphrase his recent *Business Horizons* article, a regional drug chain was highly successful over time. It built a significant competitive advantage through its founders' beliefs: customer service, friendliness, fair pricing, and a traditional health and beauty product mix. Times changed. Medical costs spiraled. Insurance companies and gov-

ernment agencies negotiated exclusive price-controlled contracts with national drug chains. Insureds were instructed to fill
their prescriptions with these chains or buy their own. Insurance companies and government agencies as third-party buyers
had become customers. National chains broadened their product lines. Hours were expanded and convenience became of
more value to many customers than service. Throughout this
time the regional chain resisted—choosing instead to intensify
its practices around the historic manifestation of its beliefs.
Recognizing the need to reinterpret how those beliefs needed to
be applied came late—perhaps too late.[13]

As a word of caution, changing ingrained, long-term behavior when the manifestation of a belief changes takes time. As
CEO Kendrick B. Melrose guided the Toro Co. back from some
bad years, he had to change the intent of a belief from "do your
job and be quiet" to "do your job and contribute to improving
it": "Some employees ... had a difficult time accepting that
management truly welcomed their ideas and had to be shaken
from the well-ingrained bureaucratic belief that silence and security walk hand-in-hand. Slowly this was accomplished
through a series of initiatives designed to solicit feedback and
recognize achievement—including monthly 'huddles' in which
'great plays' were reviewed.

"It's kind of like ... boot camp, where you immerse people
in it for so long and so intensely that they come out changed,'
Mr. Melrose says. 'But that takes a long time, and that's a long
effort.'"[14]

The review step, including monitoring and updating, brings
the basic beliefs process full circle—back around to how they
are determined.

SUMMARY

Basic beliefs play a major role in determining an organization's
success over time. If you know why you have it, success breeds
more success. Some companies never seem to rise up to the

top levels in their industries. Other companies seem on the rise at times and then fall back. Still other companies have been at the top for a long while and then begin to fade. It seems as if they didn't know what made them successful, or they knew but then lost sight of it. That can produce corporate failure: "If failure has one overarching cause, aside from patently inept management, it is the nearly incredible reality that senior executives too often don't understand the fundamentals of their business. They neglect to ask central questions, such as what precisely is their company's core expertise, what are reasonable long and short-term goals, what are the key drivers of profitability in their competitive situation. Says Stefan Fraidin, a partner at the Wall Street law firm Fried Frank Harris Shriver & Jacobson: 'It is a stunning if disturbing fact of corporate life in the 1990s: A lot of senior people at very large companies have no idea what made their organization successful.'"[15]

The companies in our survey know the power of their beliefs to make them successful over time. They also know that improving their basic beliefs process requires ongoing time and effort. They are proud of the progress made and mindful of the work yet required. The last question we asked in our survey was:

"Any other comments?"

The responses on the left show good progress in making the beliefs process work. The responses on the right show that there is still work to be done.

PROGRESS MADE	WORK REQUIRED
The Need for Beliefs	
Bottom line is the fact we all work together to give the customer the best products we possibly can using tools that make us all grow.	There is so much pressure on sales and having to meet your sales goals each month that sometimes you don't do what is best for the customer.
Thank you for creating the business climate that exists. It is the reason talented people stay.	In a conflict between political considerations and our values, politics would win most of the time.

PROGRESS MADE	WORK REQUIRED
This is the most common-sense approach to how we should deal with business issues I have ever had the privilege to be associated with.	We reward and promote those who 'get it done.' The how appears irrelevant.

How Beliefs Are Stated

Current basic beliefs are well stated.	They are too long, wordy, and trite.... They can be misinterpreted easily.
Basic beliefs are set in stone as basic beliefs.	I think the basic beliefs need to be simplified.

Communication of Beliefs

Current company beliefs are ... for the most part effectively communicated through various workshops and in meetings company-wide.	I didn't know we had basic beliefs. After the beliefs were introduced a considerable amount of time lapsed before regular communication began.

Application of Beliefs

I am proud to be part of an organization that consistently weaves the beliefs into virtually all activities in the company I've been a part of.	I believe upper management utilizes basic beliefs regularly—farther down the line I believe the passion or fire has died. The basic beliefs are a nice document, but it doesn't seem to me they are actually used.

Recognition of Beliefs Application

Overall, I believe employees try to follow the beliefs. The benefits that the employees receive really help to increase morale and dedication.	It seems we are enforcing a lack of pride, since rewards are few and far between.

Power of Beliefs

We're moving in the right direction. As a new employee, I feel good about the progress we are making and the quality of decisions, processes, etc.	I don't believe the basic beliefs are believed in. We pay little attention to them when making decisions.
It's a great program, enforcing can only make them work better, the company thrive, and the customers' needs met.	Our beliefs are still very important to the company as a whole. But sometimes I worry they are being compromised more and more as we continue to grow.

It would not surprise me to find these kinds of contrasting conclusions about basic beliefs in almost any organization. It is the intent of this book to move those "Work Required" comments to "Progress Made."

With the full basic belief process developed, it's time to explore the results that can be obtained and how to achieve them. The next four chapters describe how each of the survey companies applies basic beliefs and improves the basic beliefs process. They want their basic beliefs to guide and influence all strategic and operational decision making and action. They know that can produce a competitive advantage that will make a significant contribution to long-term, sustained growth and success.

Each story provides a different picture of the power of beliefs. They are based on interviews conducted with senior management one year after written feedback from the surveys was provided. Ben Tregoe conducted the interviews at Harley-Davidson and J. M. Smucker. I conducted them at AAA and Barnett Banks.

Sufficient description is provided so that any reader will gain a meaningful picture of what it takes to put beliefs to work. Those who want to make specific improvements in their company's basic beliefs process will find a rich and practical database from which to draw.

THE AMERICAN AUTOMOBILE ASSOCIATION

This is a story of the turnaround and unifying strength of basic beliefs in one organization. AAA is a federation. Each of the Automobile Clubs is an independent organization serving the members in its area. The Association and National Office support the needs of the Clubs and provide the "glue" that holds it all together. The effort by AAA to bring out and state their basic beliefs was documented in Chap. 3.

The American Automobile Association

BASIC BELIEFS

Preamble

Basic Beliefs are fundamental and enduring principles that guide the Association's mission, operations and corporate behavior. They are a collective commitment by Association Headquarters, clubs, employees and governing bodies to those we serve and to each other. They determine the culture of our organization; how we work with each other, our members, other customers, suppliers and the public.

• COMMITMENT TO AAA MEMBERS

We exist for our members and will judge everything we do by how well it serves their needs. AAA services, programs and products will meet the highest standards of quality and will be continually reviewed to ensure maximum member benefit. AAA services and products will be tested, proved practical and reliable and offered only to add value to membership.

- COMMITMENT TO THE ASSOCIATION

We are committed to membership growth and retention, to the federation structure and to the sovereignty of affiliated clubs. We will seek a balance between the uniformity needed to bind us together and the flexibility required to respond to local conditions. Our goal is long-term success and stability, not short-term advantage. We will devote adequate study to business and policy decisions to be confident we are acting correctly.

- COMMITMENT TO AAA EMPLOYEES

We will maintain a competently managed working environment offering fair compensation, equality in employment opportunities and potential for advancement, education and training. We will reward meritorious performance, be receptive to differing points of view and respect individual dignity.

- COMMITMENT TO COMMUNITY AND COUNTRY

We will be good corporate neighbors, engaging in public service consistent with our mission, the needs of members, the communities we serve and the national interest. In pursuing public policy positions, AAA will remain objective and responsible, relying on our credibility, expertise and research in public policy formulation.

CEO Bob Darblenet further describes the Association in terms of AAA beliefs: "Both our Clubs and National Office are well defined and have a physical presence. But the Association is less well defined, and, in fact, its form changes continually. It is probably best represented in form at the annual meeting of delegates when about 1,200 Club and National Office people get together. But when the meeting is over, the Association appears to evaporate. It may appear the following month in the form of a board or a significant committee meeting. For example, when we at the Association were focusing on the Mission of the National Office, it was a matter of defining the responsibilities and relationships between Clubs, Strategy Committees and the National Office. That relates most importantly to the intent of our beliefs about Commitment to the Association—to seek a balance between the uniformity to bind us together and the flexibility to respond to local conditions."

He further separated the uniqueness of AAA's Commitment to the Association from its other three commitments—to employees, members, community, and country: "You look at our Commitment to Employees and you could substitute another company for AAA. The same is true for members (customers) and community/country. But our fourth Commitment to the Association is most challenging. That challenge is handled by resolving the apparent contradiction between being committed to the sovereignty of the Clubs and also to the Federation structure. For example, in the past we have invested significant amounts of money in duplication that we, of course, should seek to avoid. It's only as we are effective in working together as an Association, that we can specifically fulfill our other three commitments or beliefs."

AAA's beliefs survey was completed in early 1995. From the survey results reported throughout the book, it is clear that Club CEOs took those beliefs, written in 1991, back to their Clubs and made them work in their own ways. Results were generally positive. But the survey results at the National Office level showed that not much happened with the basic beliefs there up to 1995. Top management seemed occupied with other things. Within the National Office the clear mission that should have evolved from the beliefs never materialized.

This all began to change in early 1995 with new CEO Bob Darblenet. He did not have to devise ways to revitalize the basic beliefs; they were an inherent part of his decision making and the way he managed and related to those around him. We asked Bob how he applied the beliefs on his job and across the Association: "We have spent time and effort defining more clearly what each of those statements within the basic beliefs means. We seek to set the right example—it is a lot easier to get people to focus on this type of thing if they perceive that senior executives are themselves focused on it. Another thing is to track results in terms of performance against the four beliefs. Also to reward performance based on the beliefs and to deal with nonperformance. Finally, to refer to and use the beliefs as a guide for decisions.

"For example, we have had a long-standing relationship with a particular preferred travel supplier for the benefit of our members. Competition among various travel suppliers is heating up. Each has been taking a more aggressive approach with various partners they do business with like AAA. They are trying to prevent those partners from having too close a relationship with competing travel suppliers. We were in the process of establishing a more formal relationship with that supplier. They threw into the negotiation a requirement that would limit our ability to promote other suppliers to our members. There were rewards to AAA to accept that. But when it came to making the decision, we were guided by our Commitment to our Members—'We exist for our members and will judge everything we do by how well it serves their needs.' Restrictions on our ability to inform our members of the benefits they are entitled to from other suppliers would be inappropriate."

In his initial address to AAA at the April 1995 Annual Meeting, Bob outlined his thinking and plans using AAA's four basic belief Commitments—to Members, the Association, Employees, and Community and Country. That set the stage. When we interviewed him in October 1996, he said: "With regard to both setting strategy and addressing operational issues, we need the commitment of our employees. We will be reaching out through them to the Clubs we serve, and we need the highest caliber employees to obtain the commitment to this organization which is necessary. Reciprocally, our Commitment to Employees is of highest priority."

Wayne Campton, Managing Director of Quality and Education, continues: "Bob took the survey reports to heart ... and through word and deed communicated to his direct reports and to the senior management team that this was a key issue that needed to be dealt with in short order. He asked his management team to work with their respective staffs to do an assessment of the underlying problems and root causes and to suggest action plans. We did that. It was very rigorous, and we spent many long weeks involving every level of the organization."

From that database, Bob went to work on the Commitment to Employees. He took each belief in that Commitment and published what he expected to happen to the entire National Office staff in September 1995. For example, in regard to *competently managed work environment* he said: "Issues identified through the Employee Climate Survey will be addressed in a timely manner. Departments showing substandard Employee Climate Survey results will be closely monitored. A summary climate survey will be conducted for those areas in January 1996. A full national office climate survey will be conducted annually. A clear indication of improvement will be a fundamental requirement for incumbent management." In regard to *fair compensation* he wrote: "National office salary scales will be reviewed and adjusted to ensure that AAA's compensation policy is competitive with target market for all levels. Performance appraisal systems and procedures will be revised to ensure that performance appraisals are reflective of actual performance. Compensation increases will be administered to ensure that AAA's relative competitiveness to target market is uniform for all levels. It is intended that funding for the above initiatives will be within the scope of national office operating budget. Operating cost reduction measures will be required to provide the necessary additional funds."

He gave the same level of thought and detail to the other sub-beliefs in the Commitment to Employees: *equality of employment opportunities, potential for advancement, education and training, reward meritorious performance, be receptive to differing points of view,* and *respect individual dignity.*

He then went to work to clarify the purpose of the National Office. His first step was to gather information. He asked the key stakeholders—the Association Board, the National Office staff, and the Clubs—what they felt the role of the National Office should be in supporting the Association; the individual Clubs; and, through the Clubs, their members. Working with key stakeholders, he clarified and simplified the Association Vision and the National Office Mission:

"Association Vision. AAA membership provides security, value and peace of mind through automotive, travel, and associated services.

National Office Mission. We exist to support the Clubs in their efforts to serve their members. We will do for the Clubs those things which can be done more effectively on a collective basis."

That mission statement came directly from AAA's beliefs about its commitment to members and commitment to the association.

Five objectives were formulated to implement the National Office Mission. Key Result Areas were developed for each objective. Specific goals in terms of projects and activities were set for each Key Result Area. To illustrate using the first objective:

NATIONAL OFFICE

OBJECTIVES	KEY RESULT AREAS	GOALS
1. Leverage the collective power of the clubs and their members	Proprietary products and services	Create a uniform membership card/credit card
	Purchasing	Offer worldwide access to member services
	Partnering and alliances	Expand member options for access to AAA services and products

To cover all five objectives, eighteen Key Result Areas were identified, with thirty specific National Office Goals.

A process to monitor progress on Commitment to Employees was put into place. A 1996 Status Report states what to track and the status for each of the beliefs under Commitment to Employees. Current status is really what has been done and what needs doing. To illustrate using one belief, *fair compensation*:

NATIONAL OFFICE MANAGEMENT PRIORITIES

STATUS REPORT, SEPTEMBER 1996

MANAGEMENT PRIORITY	TRACKING METHOD	STATUS
I. Commitment to Employees		
b. Fair Compensation	Annual Salary Scale Review	(Omitted)
	Performance Appraisal	New appraisal form to be reviewed during 4th quarter with revisions to be implemented in January 1997. Preparations being made for common review date in April 1997.
	Competitive Compensation Increases	(Omitted)
	Compensation Costs within Budget	(Omitted)

Similar detailing was given to the other beliefs under Commitment to Employees: *competently managed work environment, equality of employment opportunities, potential for advancement, education and training, reward meritorious performance, be receptive to differing points of view,* and *respect individual dignity.*

The purpose of the new performance appraisal program mentioned in the status report is clearly stated on the appraisal form: "To evaluate performance and provide management with a basis of planning a program of performance development with the employee. The performance appraisal and compensation program will be driven by and reflect AAA's values and key result areas as indicated in our Mission Statement and Basic Beliefs." Not surprisingly, the new performance appraisal reports for both management and all nonmanagement National Office staff include a specific Core Criterion to evaluate support for Basic Beliefs regarding Members, Association, Employees, and Community. All the other Core Criteria in Section 1 of the form relate to the Commitment to Employees. They include: Human Resource Management, Information Flow and Communication, Leadership through Teamwork, and Relationship Building. Section 2 of the form covers the implementation of the National Office Mission. The Core Criteria are: Quality Management and Customer Service, Innovation, Problem Solving/Decision Making, and Relevance of Activities (relevance to the Mission). Section 3 of the form covers the Management of Productivity and Costs.

Section II of the Status Report relates to progress on implementing the National Office Mission:

NATIONAL OFFICE MANAGEMENT PRIORITIES

STATUS REPORT, SEPTEMBER 1996

MANAGEMENT PRIORITY	TRACKING METHOD	STATUS
II. Relevance and Quality of Activities		
a. Relevance	National Office activities link directly to National Office Mission and Objectives	Evaluation ongoing in 1996. Club and Internal Customer Satisfaction Survey results help track relevance
b. Quality	Meet or exceed club expectations in quality and timeliness of delivery. Prepare action plans to address concerns	Measure by Club Satisfaction Survey completed January 1996

We asked Bob Darblenet if the basic beliefs, through all this action, were related to the bottom line: "The answer is yes. Starting with our Commitment to Employees, and this may be overused, to the extent that you take care of your employees you take care of your customers. If you will, you can't expect employees to treat your customers any better than you treat them. It is through being attentive to our Commitment to Employees that I believe we insure that the organization will have a healthy bottom line. If we are not attentive to fulfilling our beliefs about employees and helping Clubs fulfill their Commitment to Members, we are going to see that reflected in renewal rates, new member growth rates, and business volume with any member. So, beliefs have a definite link to the bottom line."

Wayne Campton comments on the difference in National Office purpose before and after early 1995: "In the past, the National Office would often determine Association priorities and set direction. We would strongly influence which initiatives the Association would undertake and what products and services to offer. When Bob arrived he posed this question, 'If the National Office did not exist, would there be a need for one and, if there was a need, what would that be?' And the answers: be customer driven—to serve the needs of the Clubs, in terms of products, services, and support, to enable Clubs to better serve their members. And to do things that are most effectively done on a collective basis. That change in Mission was like night and day."

We spoke with Carol Dressler, Managing Director of Human Resources, about what happened to basic beliefs violators: "Where we have had managers who were not really living up to our basic beliefs as far as employees, we worked with these folks to give them an opportunity to get up to speed. When they were not able to, we have had demotions. When any employee does not live up to our basic belief about members, that is grounds for termination."

She explained what AAA does to get impact on a "softer" employee sub-belief like *be receptive to differing points of view* and *respect individual dignity*: "We now require National Office staff meetings be held once a month, with a staff officer present at least quarterly, to exchange information between employees and management. It is the employees' opportunity to say what they like and dislike about what we are doing. Suggestions are encouraged and acted on. We have mandatory courses for managers. One deals with civil treatment. It explores diversity, how you respect cultural differences, and just how to work with people to respect their dignity. The course explains how to adapt to different styles so judgments aren't made on the basis of those differences.

"We are introducing 360-degree feedback at management levels. An outside firm handles the program. They provide and interpret the evaluation forms. Each participant is given five forms for peers, five for subordinates, and one for supervisor and self. The participant decides who to give them to. Guidance is provided for those decisions. The participant receives a confidential summary via computer. No individual respondents are identified. It is strictly a developmental tool. Training resources and programs are available, but it is up to each participant to map out his or her own program and use whatever resources desired. If any participant wants one, counselors are available. I would like to receive overall feedback on general areas of development so we can create programs and opportunities to fill them. But, that is for the future.

"We have also changed the compensation system. We reduced salary grades from 28 to 18 and broadened the range in each grade. We also made the range of equal breadth at all 18 levels. It used to broaden as you went up the line. This lets people work and be rewarded in grade rather than always having to push to get up a grade. We also will implement an incentive system for all National Office employees. Those incentives will be based on three criteria: satisfying our customers (the Clubs), fulfilling our Commitment to Employees, and financial results. The first two are truly based on our beliefs."

Bob, Wayne, and Carol all commented in the same general way when asked how progress on Commitment to Employees and the implementation of the National Office Mission will be measured. Beyond the formal individual performance appraisal program described above, progress will basically be measured by two surveys. The Club Satisfaction Survey is conducted every year. This survey is completed by each Club and assesses the degree to which the National Office is accomplishing its Mission and applying beliefs in so doing. It is very detailed, with frequent comparisons to the previous survey and to world-class benchmark companies.

The 1995 survey results are significantly better than those from 1993 in these areas: overall satisfaction, satisfaction with various National Office departments, leadership (close to world-class), communications, seeking and utilizing Club input, and trust. The overall Club CEO satisfaction with the National Office on achieving its Mission went from 53 percent in 1993 to 85 percent in 1995. The average satisfaction for all departments is up 10 percent, to 69 percent. Clubs rated the importance of and satisfaction with all of the National Office Key Result Areas in the Mission Statement. The gaps between importance and satisfaction give the National Office feedback on where improvement is required. Finally, the Clubs rated every National Office department—21 in total—on the products and services they provide to Clubs. Club write-in comments on improving communication and trust were extensive.

The second survey is an Employee Climate Survey completed once each year within the National Office. This analysis compares the 1995 and 1996 selected results from 600-plus responses. A five-point scale was used with each question—strongly agree, agree, neutral or no opinion, disagree, strongly disagree. The "positive" percent is the average of all responses to the two positive categories. The "negative" percent is for the two negative categories. The positive and negative change from 1995 to 1996 is shown.

AAA EMPLOYEE CLIMATE SURVEY COMPARISON

SELECTED QUESTIONS	1995 TO 1996 PERCENTAGE CHANGE	
	POSITIVE	NEGATIVE
8. My management does a good job of recognizing employee contributions to improving customer service.	+27	−10
27. I have a good understanding of the following:		
a) National Office Mission Statement - - - - - - - - -	+9	NC
b) Overall organization objectives for the National Office -	+17	NC
c) Steps we are taking as an organization to reach the objectives of the National Office - - - - - - - -	+35	+4

SELECTED QUESTIONS	*1995 TO 1996* PERCENTAGE CHANGE	
	POSITIVE	NEGATIVE
31. To what extent are overall practices at the National Office consistent with the Basic Beliefs?		
a) Commitment to AAA Members - - - - - - - - - - -	+21	−6
b) Commitment to the Association - - - - - - - - - - -	+26	−4
c) Commitment to AAA Employees - - - - - - - - - -	+29	−25
d) Commitment to Community/Country - - - - - - -	+4	NC
55. I think my performance on the job is evaluated fairly. -	+17	−2
69. To what extent is the management of the National Office interested in the welfare and overall satisfaction for all of the people who work here? - -	+25	−18
72. To what extent do you trust that your best interests are taken into account by your immediate supervisor? -	+16	−10
77. Overall, taking everything into account, how satisfied are you with the AAA National Office as an organization to work for? - - - - - - - - - - - - - - -	+25	NC

Both surveys stress in many ways the importance of and improvements in trust. In a federation, trust is the linchpin for melding the independence of the Clubs with the overall governance of the Association and the National Office. It is enhanced through open and honest communication.

Bob stresses the critical role of the Association-level committees in that communication/trust evolution. There are three such committees and they are composed of rotating Club and Association members and report to the corporate board. The strategy committee determines what businesses AAA should be in and where it should head. That provides a product/service development base for the National Office. A second committee works on quality improvement, that has to do with accreditation procedures for Clubs, moving quality standards toward world-class level, and the like. A third committee guides AAA public policy and government relations. Bob is the bridge between the output of those committees and the work of the Association and National Office in supporting the Clubs.

Bob commented on what he does to gain application of beliefs at Club level: "Communicate the beliefs, define them more clearly, refer to them in decisions. But we have to be mindful that we don't have our own shop entirely in order at the National Office level. Before we attempt to preach to the Clubs that they ought to make sure they are adhering to the basic beliefs, I believe strongly that we need to improve our performance in that regard."

We asked Carol about the value of all of these approaches tied to basic beliefs and carrying that message through to the Clubs: "This is one of the things we are working on right now. There are a lot of resources that we have here and many Clubs are very sophisticated with their own programs. We are looking at the computer as a way to open channels across the organization; to be able to share all programs and ideas both ways. In the next few weeks the Clubs and National Office staffs will get together and share training materials, programs, and any approaches that have proven effective. This is a new kind of shared effort. It is not formalized yet but we hope to be there within a year."

All of these approaches show that at AAA basic beliefs are in place to become the drivers of strategic and operational decision making. While this progress on the basic beliefs process is exciting in its potential impact on long-term sustained growth and employee and member satisfaction, it is still in an early stage. Wayne ended his interview with a realistic caution: "Bob Darblenet has worked the basic beliefs process so that all his direct reports and senior management 'walk the talk.' That is spreading down through the organization. But if for some unfortunate reason Bob were not here, some may have a tendency to revert back to old ways of doing business, and that's a tough one."

You don't become a "visionary company" overnight. When basic beliefs become the way to set future product and market strategy, to accomplish work, to treat and relate to each other, and to share the bounties, then an organization can cope with any change and stay on course for long-term sustained success.

HARLEY-DAVIDSON, INC.

According to Chairman and CEO Rich Teerlink, this is a story of renewal—of bringing Harley-Davidson back to the enviable position it holds today. First, the company experienced a turn-around driven by crisis and survival. Then, sustained renewal was driven by a set of basic values that underlie strategic and operational decision making, as expressed in a working document entitled the Business Process.

HARLEY-DAVIDSON, INC.
BUSINESS PROCESS

VALUES		ISSUES		STAKEHOLDERS
Tell the Truth		Quality		All those inside or
•		• Continuous improvement		outside an organization
Be Fair		activities to reduce waste,		who are directly
•		defects, and variability in		affected by what it
Keep Your		everything we do, while		does:
Promises		striving to meet & exceed		
•		customer expectations		Customers
Respect the				•
Individual	↔	Participation	↔	Suppliers
•		• Is open to influence;		•
Encourage		Provides an opportunity		Employees
Intellectual Curiosity		to make a difference		•
				Investors
		Productivity		•
		• Is Effective: Does the		Governments
		Right Thing		•
		• Is Efficient: Does the		Society
		Thing Right		

(Continued on next page)

(Continued from previous page)

Flexibility
- Rapidly and efficiently
responds to changes
in the internal and
external environment
Cash Flow
- The necessity for longevity
↓

Vision

Harley-Davidson is an action-oriented, international company, a leader in its commitment to continuously improve our mutually beneficial relationships with stakeholders. Harley-Davidson believes the key to success is to balance stakeholders' interests through the empowerment of all employees to focus on value-added activities.
↓

Mission
↓
Operating Philosophies
↓
Objectives
Strategic and Financial
↓
Circle/Function
Strategy
↓
Work Unit Plans
↓
My Job

Rich tells the story: "One of the things that was consistent all along the line was a small core of dedicated customers who had been abused. They had been sold products that didn't work, products that leaked oil, and at prices significantly higher than the market. Perhaps management thought that profits were the most important thing. When AMF decided to sell the company, nobody wanted it. In a leveraged buyout, they sold it to a group of employees led by then Chairman Vaughn L. Beals Jr. That was in June of 1981. That group recognized that they had to have products that work, and had the latent power of all these people who wanted to own Harleys. All we had to do was give them an opportunity to buy them.

"I came two months after the buyout. The turnaround of 1981 was survival. Number one, we had to design products that worked. Number two, we had to manufacture products of high quality. Number three, we had to use the power of our brand to go out there and sell this product.

"We went public in July of 1986. By that time, obviously we were through the turnaround, though we weren't as far along as most people thought. When you come out of the survival mode, everyone takes a deep breath and relaxes. What we really had to do was come up with a vehicle at that point that focused on the issue of renewal.

"We started talking about these kinds of things, calling it the Business Process, in 1988, and actually formalized it in 1989. We didn't do it with a lot of hoopla. We sort of let it sit and let people hear about it and talk about it, but not a full-court press. We wanted to give it a gestation period."

Rich explained how the Business Process developed: "I had a concept that we should have some systematic way of dealing with how the business operates. I think where we are today is the outcome of a lot of fits and starts at what's good and what's bad. I had something to do with it. I was the initial driver behind it. Today I'm not the driver. It is where it should be—part of the fabric of the organization.

"I think a lot of what we did was just to codify some of the things that were here already—but to make us more accountable to them. We put in five values to apply to five issues. When you don't have them articulated you end up with many overlapping values—you say the same thing seventeen times and you've got forty-three values. What we have said is, 'Tell the truth, be fair,'—fairly straightforward—almost 'Baseball, Chevrolet, and Apple Pie.' And I know that's the way. Imagine a world that lived by those values. Imagine an organization that could live by them. Think of the value-added time we would add to the organization if we weren't worried about those kinds of values being practiced. The focus on values is the major thing that impacts the five issues. If we can get those issues right—quality, participation, productivity, flexibility, and cash flow—we are halfway down the line."

Bill Gray, Vice President of Human Resources, comments: "The Business Process is largely Rich. He is a tremendous visionary, and he could look up and see where this business needed to be and what it needed to have to get there. Jeff [Jeff Bleustein, President and COO] is tremendously analytical, a very bright guy, and he was able to see the importance of the application of this. And these two guys have done it."

We talked about how the Business Process was built into the organization. One of the conclusions from our survey was that the importance of the Business Process was felt more strongly at higher levels than further down the line. At the time of the survey, that was true. But things have changed. Rich spoke of his responsibility: "I saw we were not having effective communication. So what I've done is delegate to the functional leadership group the responsibility for designing and delivering Business Process modules. The first course was on values. We got the attention of senior leaders not to do lip service. They had to present their module to Jeff and me so we could see what they were doing. It is my job to carry this through to those who work in my realm, but I'm sort of a carrier of the message and not an implementer with the rest of the workforce."

Bill adds: "They put this together and they take a great deal of interest and a strong hand in developing these courses. It's not that we have some instructional desire. Senior leadership of the business designed the courses and Jeff and Rich have their fingerprints all over each one. They are intensely interested in getting this out."

Then Rich talked of the communication process through the salaried levels: "The modules were an attempt to take the whole Business Process and waterfall it through the organization with the leaders talking with their first reports. All of the members of the senior management group had to present a four-hour session to their first reports on what values mean. A crucial part of it, that I think is important for leaders to do, is to step up and say, 'This is what this means to me and how am I doing?'

"Their first reports had to do it for their first reports—it cascaded down through the organization. What is fascinating is, to my knowledge, none of those meetings lasted only four hours.

They went longer, and it was because it gave an opportunity for communication about this important thing called values. How do they fit in what we do here in our everyday work life? I am told by employees that this was one of the most meaningful forms of communication they ever had with their leader.

"Then we did a module on each other part of the Business Process. Now this is spread throughout the whole salaried workforce."

Bill provides more detail on the development and implementation of the Business Process modules: "In trying to discover how we could translate some of the softer values into action, we got set back in thought. Maybe we should be teaching courses, values as a course, and issues, the whole Business Process as a series of courses and identified behaviors that we believe are consistent with those values. What does the company mean when it says, 'Tell the truth?' Let's define it. What behaviors are there?

"I'll describe the course on values. It's laid out as to what you do and what you say. But we stimulate a dialog with our people, and you can imagine a room of ten or twelve people and a leader talking about the definition of 'tell the truth.' To provide full and accurate representation of the facts about a situation is what we mean by telling the truth. What behaviors are attended to that? It confronts the issues fully. That's what this corporation expects: If you are going to tell the truth you'll confront issues fully and be open, honest, and objective. The functional leader will teach this to his or her direct reports and then those leaders teach it to the next level because we want the interaction to be between leader and employees. They're starting to contract with each other on the Business Process."

Next Rich talked about the Business Process with dealers: "I have spoken at dealer meetings with a very complete description of the Business Process. I am always talking and referring to it at every dealer meeting and every Harley-Davidson University, which is where we train our dealers in three one-week sessions during the winter."

Bill further describes how Harley-Davidson values are reinforced with their dealers: "I'm teaching a course at the next dealer conference, which is in January. We're bringing in all our dealers. Part of that experience together will be merchandising and a parts and accessories show. The other part is education. One of the subjects being offered is the Business Process with a specific section on values and issues as related to stakeholder interests. And my colleague Ron Hutchinson is VP of parts and accessories and we will be team teaching the course six times. This is the first time with dealers. We are going to encourage them to look at their own values in terms of running their own business and what relationship they think that means with their customers, employees, and suppliers."

Rich continues with Harley-Davidson's suppliers: "Next week at our supplier conference I will talk once again about the issue of a mutually beneficial relationship. We have a supplier visit program. During each of those meetings one member of the Harley-Davidson management team discusses our Business Process and values. We try to make it part of our everyday talk."

Bill cites a very specific example of the impact of Harley-Davidson values on supplier relationships: "We work with our suppliers and tend to encourage a long-term relationship. There are times, of course, when a supplier relationship may start to sour. And rather than just cut it off, like many companies would, we go in and work with that supplier. We've got to be fair. We've got to talk to them and share our sense of the problem and then also share our expertise on the fix. It's not uncommon for us to send engineers to a vendor and help them solve the manufacturing problem so they can continue to be a valued supplier to our business. That's proven to be very rewarding. I know that many purchasing people around the world say, 'Well, if he can't supply them, I'll just go over here.' Our company is not like that. I saw one decision turned around. Our buyer decided to terminate a vendor and our vice president of purchasing said, 'Well let's test your decision against the values. Have you done that?' 'No sir, I have not.' 'Then you're not going to terminate the vendor. I want you to go work with them. We will be fair. If ultimately the problem can't be solved, terminate the relationship.'"

We asked Rich about building the Business Process into the hourly employee group: "Jeff and I talked to over one hundred labor leaders in our partnering process, which is building a mutually beneficial relationship. When we are done, everyone in the organization will have spent a significant amount of time talking about the Business Process, but, more importantly, seeing opportunities to live it, not just have it done with a plaque on the wall. We have gone into these partnership agreements with our labor unions at all of our plants. When we made the presentation to the leadership of the planning groups for the partnering agreements, they were very excited about the Business Process. In fact, they said it's got to be in our education system."

Bill gets very specific on how the values and Business Process are putting a fresh, new, positive light on union–management relationships: "What I've tried to do in labor negotiations and normal employee relations is constantly cause us to test what we're doing and what we're saying against the Business Process. Because we are practicing it together, labor is starting to find out that this stuff does work: that the Business Process is meaningful; that it is not a tool of management that you begrudgingly go with; that, in fact, it opens our minds to mutual problem resolution. So, we are sinking our teeth into that and are now hearing labor leaders in our business saying, 'Let's test our decision against the balancing of stakeholders' interests. Are we mutually benefiting the various stakeholders? Oh, we can't do that because it's penalizing this factor or that factor. Let's get creative and determine how we can do something different.'

"Rich and Jeff went with me to visit the international presidents of the Machinists and the United Paper Workers. In that meeting the four leaders talked about their vision of a new era of labor–management relations based on the Business Process and the values that unions hold dear. As a result of those discussions we have formed a partnership with those two unions. We have jointly selected the new plant site. We have jointly determined how to staff that business. We've jointly determined what product to put in that plant. Labor and management in those decisions have been part of the same team. And we're helping the union carry the message to other union people. You don't have to have an adversarial relationship. We can be very successful together if we understand and respect each other's institutions. If we are fair and respectful to the union situation, they are respectful and fair to the company. It's a win-win."

Bill describes how the Business Process is built into the Harley-Davidson annual leadership meeting. That meeting involves three hundred employees including management, union leadership, plant personnel, and representatives from the Asian and European operations: "The Business Process was shown on the screen a number of times. We related the strategic plan and various financial and nonfinancial objectives to the Business Process to show what we're trying to accomplish over the long run. We've brought it down to how does this drive your own work unit plans and your own commitments. But let's look back and understand the way these strategies are played off against our values, issues, and stakeholders and the mutually beneficial relationships that we believe need to be continually enhanced."

In our survey, one of the comments was: "Who runs the company? We never see them!" Rich mentioned that at their October 1996 annual leadership meeting a similar question was raised. When we asked him about this, he had a very thoughtful and penetrating response: "That means out in the plants, on the floor, out in the field. Part of the answer is me. I want to add value when I go somewhere. So, to go to a plant and walk through down the main aisle waving at everybody to me is just phony. I said at the meeting, 'I've never turned down an invitation to go anywhere.' I have met with many departments and groups of employees because they have asked me to. I think it gets back to something called individual responsibility. If that's bugging you, don't complain. Call the people you want to see and say come out here and let's talk. I would rather have that, than have people say we saw him walk through last week."

We asked Rich if he thought people would really do that: "Why not? Our Business Process is based on individual responsibility. The bottom of the Process is My Job. So, in there is the opportunity for people to make that happen.

"What do I do? Once a month Jeff and I spend an hour and a half with new employees at new employee orientation. We go to conferences. We go to meetings inside. We walk into the lunchroom. I will randomly sit down at tables, occasionally. I have a problem doing that. That's their free time. I don't think it's a smart thing for me to do. So I am trying hard to say to the leadership of the organization—look, if you want us and your employees don't think they see us enough, you have a responsibility to ask us. The plant manager down at York did that, and I did eight two-hour sessions with all the employees at York."

Bill cited a specific example he was involved in with the application of values: "The senior leadership of our business was faced with making some changes to our retiree health care plan in order to cut some of our future expenses. We had resolved to take one approach that we felt would be the right thing for the business, and we were going to go forward with it. But one of us raised the issue of testing it against our values. It didn't pass the test. It wasn't fair to people who invested their whole lives in Harley-Davidson and served us well. And so we went back to the drawing board. We changed our decision before we had ever taken it to the street. We said, 'How do we make it fair?' The plan that we ultimately developed was very highly regarded by our people. It made some positive changes for them in retiring health care. It also put a cap on the company's liability. And the company and our future retirees came out winners and our stakeholders were well served."

Rich explained how he measured the degree of importance employees placed on the Business Process: "There are several ways. At the annual leadership conference, in talking about a number of items, the Business Process came up frequently. When I talk with people about a project, they tell me how it sits with the Business Process. We set up our compensation system so it supports our values. I see things in the policies that say we run the organization by the Business Process and the things we normally do to support it. I think we are trying to have a freer organization with regard to talking with one another."

We asked Bill and Rich if the values and Business Process have a direct impact on the bottom line, and how. First Bill comments: "If you understand the process—we have values, issues, stakeholders, the vision, objectives and strategies, work unit plans, and my job. Each step further specifies the previous step. I'm expected to write my commitments for my job in terms of how they fit the work unit plan. If my colleagues and I are doing an excellent job of that, the strategies get accomplished. And, assuming the strategies drive growth in the business and earnings, then, of course it goes straight to the bottom line. We're seeing people do more with this and we're seeing people focused in on that work unit plan and their involvement with it. And they can look at the Business Process chart and see how it plays right to where this business is trying to go. It ties us all together in a common direction and harnesses an awful lot of force. I've seen hourly people do this, salaried people as well. And we have productivity increases as a result that translate to profitability."

Then Rich takes over: "I think where we are different is the umbrella of the Business Process that sets the context for the business and tries to make the direct connection on the part of the employee to the total thing that is going on. Not just, 'I'm here working in accounts payable and my job is to process invoices.' No. No. No. 'My job is to add value and how do I do that?'

"If we follow all the steps in the Business Process down to work unit plans, the leader of that work unit has an obligation to define why this department exists. He must help each employee understand it and how he or she serves the department's job. So, in the ideal world everybody understands everything they have to about their job and work unit, but more importantly they understand the direction of the company, and most important the environment in which the company wants to operate. I'm a firm believer that the leaders are responsible for that environment, and the Business Process is the key element that creates that environment. When people come into work they say, 'I know what I've got to do, I know how I can do it, and I know how I'm going to get rewarded.' Does it work 100 percent of the time? Absolutely not!"

Bill supports that idea: "There are occasions when our actions do not fit the Business Process, specifically our values expectations. This is an evolutionary process, and we all goof at some point in time. I'm sure I've done things that in my mind are fair that other people feel are unfair. Among the leadership groups we're trying to say, 'If you catch me doing something that appears contrary to our values call it to my attention at the time so we can deal with it.' I'd rather deal with it at the moment than have it fester."

Bill explains how employees are rewarded for application of the Business Process: "Individual performance links to the work unit, which links all the way back up to the values. Each employee is to develop personal commitments for each year of performance, and people are rewarded on the basis of bringing home those commitments. So they are rewarded for the Business Process in their merit increases. Our bonus program is not individually driven. You might enjoy a larger percentage of your base as a target for your bonus than I do. That's based on your position in the organization. But when the bonus numbers come out, we all get the same percentage of target: if you're getting paid 90% of target, I'm getting paid 90% of target. So senior leaders are not accumulating wealth disproportionate to others' opportunities. We just don't work it that way."

We asked Bill if there were specific financial rewards for an outstanding application of the values and the Business Process: "Nothing tied specifically to this. If people are living the Business Process, they're probably doing very well at their jobs, and they are the ones you tend to want to accelerate. You want to promote them and give them new and broader responsibilities. Those are the people that are rising up in the organization. Those that do not live our values and use the Business Process tend to be those that aren't performing well, and those people we're encouraging out of the organization."

There are ways for employees to report up the line something happening in opposition to the Business Process. Rich explains: "They all have that opportunity to do so whenever they want to. Some do and some don't. But that's typical of any organization. Do we have too much? I don't know. But I do know when employees get upset enough I've had them come directly to me because they were afraid of the system. And we talk about it. It gets put right back into the system, and every one of those problems has been solved, and the employee is happy with the solution."

How do you create shareholder value and how do you deal with the investment community and pressures for short-term results? Rich responds: "First thing we do whenever we are out is state honestly and openly that we do not run our business for shareholder value in the short-run. We run it for long-term shareholder value. Whenever we do a presentation, including those with security analysts, I've gone through the Business Process umbrella—explaining this is the environmental context of how we run our business. We get arguments from them. I'm not out to evangelize. I believe strongly in this. You may take a different approach. I think it works pretty well because the relationship we have with our customers recognizes them as very, very important stakeholders, not a revenue source. That is a dramatic difference because they carry on the heritage and legacy of this company. My job is to develop the approach to leadership that allows the legacy to continue. Those who came before started the customer bonding that saw us through thick and thin. We must recognize that, while considering the importance of all other stakeholders too.

"There is too much measuring of financial results rather than what's been done. If you get good, long-term financial results you have to ask yourself where it's coming from. We happen to think a lot of our good performance is coming from the environment we've tried to create through the Business Process. A lot of things support this—our compensation system, the way we are organized, our lifelong learning program. They all fit in. Our partnering with our unions would not be here today if we did not believe in that concept. Some people could say, 'Well, you're partnering with the union to get a better deal.' Not at all. We think we can have a mutually beneficial relationship. It's the best deal we can have if we're all concerned about long-term value added."

Bill expands on Rich's point that the Business Process strongly influenced the way Harley-Davidson is organized to manage the business: "We've now taken the Business Process one step beyond. We've said that there needs to be a unique way to practice some of this stuff so we've created an organization of three interlocking, cross-functional, interdependent circles. We have a Create Demand circle, a Produce Products circle, and a Provide Support circle. Now, in a normal organization, these would be reflected in a stick-and-box kind of organization chart, but we've got senior leaders that have membership on each one of these circles and they overlap. This is our system of governance and it relates directly to the Business Process—bringing it to life and making it a part of our everyday lives. And hopefully, through example, others will catch on—we're seeing circles, cross-functional circles, extend down through the organization." A graphic of this organization appears on page 132.

The Circles report to the president. He, along with Circle members, determines rotating membership, compensation, and career development of members. He reviews each Circle's commitments and resulting assessments.

Bill provides an uplifting summary to this story: "I think the Business Process has another very large benefit for this company because it provides an ordered way for all of us to think about the company. It brings in all aspects of the company. And it's simple. It's simple to visualize. It's simple to remember what's in those circles and boxes and in each stage of the Business Process. Our values are just five and they're simple. We only have five issues. Everything we do relates to those values and issues.

"There's plenty of room for individual capabilities and individual experiences. It plays to diversity in our business. It helps

Harley-Davidson Motor Company

SENIOR LEADERSHIP ELEMENTS
OF THE ORGANIZATION
THE CIRCLES

The Motor Company is divided into three broad functional areas called Circles. These Circles are: Create Demand, Produce Product and Provide Support. Each Circle is composed of the leaders representing specific functions within it. For example, the Produce Products Circle contains Engineering, Powertrain Operations, York, Tomahawk, Purchasing, Quality, and Kansas City.

Functional areas within Circles may change from time to time. The current Circles and their specific functions are:

Business Development
Customer Service
General Mdse. Mktg.
Motorcycle and P&A Mktg.
Sales—Americas
Styling
HD-Europe
HD-Asia Pacific
Trade/Regulatory Affairs

Engineering & Talladega
Powertrain Operations
York Operations
Tomahawk Operations
Purchasing
Quality
Logistics
Kansas City Operations

Finance
Human Resources
Legal
Information Services
Communications
Strategic Planning

Circle Governance

Each Circle will operate as an empowered work team. We do not expect a single individual to emerge as the Circle leader. Rather, we expect the leadership role to move to different individuals as a function of the issue being addressed.

Updated October 21, 1996

us recognize why we have to be aware of diversity and respond to people who are different, whether it's color or creed or whatever. It allows us to think so much more differently about where each individual fits into the business, what kind of players we are and how we can help the business be successful.

"I see the senior leadership here living the values. And I've been in other companies where the leader will articulate the values, but they're not something he lives. There hasn't been a leadership commitment to 'walking the talk' as people say. I hate that term, but people understand what it is. They haven't been committed to living up to things that their company believes in.

"I'm working with a couple of pretty unique guys. I've never been in a place where senior leadership is fond of each other. We really enjoy working together. It is fun being together with these twenty-one other people. There's a genuine liking which I've not seen in other companies. If we're living our values, I'm not going to stab you in the back. I'm going to help you with your problem, and you'll value me even more because I've helped you with your problem or you've helped me. And when we have this kind of cross-functional interdependence, it's a fun environment because we're not competing against anybody except the outside world. And so we can have fun with each other. We get mad at each other, but it's never taken personally. I truly enjoy my colleagues and I think they enjoy me."

Now, Harley-Davidson faces major decisions to sustain and extend its success. It must appease customers who wait for their bikes. It must fight off new Japanese competitors. It must energize its dealer network to broaden customer service to take better advantage of current strengths. It must significantly expand production while keeping and improving quality and controlling costs. It must gear up to tailor and expand overseas business.

There seems little doubt that if Harley-Davidson continues to increase the application of its competencies, as contained in its values and the Business Process, Rich, Jeff, Bill, and all the others will conquer these decisions. They will sustain and increase long-term value added for all stakeholders. They will become a "visionary company" in the fullest sense. Time will tell.

If you invested $100 in Harley-Davidson, Inc. common stock on July 15, 1986, the date they went public, and reinvested all the dividends, the value of your investment on December 31, 1995 would be $2,122.

BARNETT BANKS, INC.

This is the story of a fast-growing regional service company in the relationship business. They have many separate facilities and a desire to knit all of their employees into a smoothly functioning team. Paul Kerins, Chief Human Resources Executive, reviews the history: "In 1992, we were wrestling with concerns around further enhancing our commitment to quality service. It became clear to us that companies that went to the next level in terms of quality were those that took time to establish a vision. To start putting in specific programs in isolation didn't work—they had no staying power. So the Management Operating Committee went off in early 1993, to do some team building and to come away with a vision. That included a statement of mission or fundamental purpose and an Operating Vision or a set of beliefs to guide the accomplishment of that purpose. Implementation will be through specific operating strategies each developed by a goal team. We brought it back and tested whether it felt right with a number of different audiences within the company."

A meeting was held in early 1994 to introduce the newly formulated vision to those who would serve on the goal teams and plan the specific operating strategies. Charles Rice, Chairman and CEO, began the meeting by explaining the fundamental mission of the company: "We intend to create value for our owners, customers, and employees as a highly profitable, independent, financial services organization in markets where we have a leadership position."

Allen Lastinger, President and COO, described Barnett's Operating Vision or basic beliefs. First he read the simple statement:

- We are Barnett, the nationally recognized standard in the financial services industry.
- Barnett people are caring and proud.
- We improve the lives of our customers and the well-being of our communities.
- We help each other succeed, and we make our customers feel like they belong!
- We are team Barnett!

He spoke to the first ambitious belief: "I realize it's somewhat presumptuous to include the phrase 'nationally recognized standard.' We know we are not there yet, but we firmly believe that if we don't aspire to be the best we never will be. We must focus on those businesses that play to our strengths and then operate better than our competitors."

As far as Barnett people, he talked of improving the quality of work life. He put the focus on building the team: "By helping each other and caring for each other, each member of the team wins." In this context, he mentioned that a recent question asked why the word employee is not in the vision: "We did not want to create a vision of a company that was hierarchical. When we say Barnett people help each other, we are focusing on how we support each other and what we need to do for the team. It is meant to view caring across a broad range of relationships."

He spoke of anticipating customer needs and providing service to exceed their expectations. As far as leadership, he talked of the important role Barnett employees played in their community.

He concluded: "Over the next week, we will be having similar meetings for regional Barnett employees. After that, division heads will begin the process in each division. These meetings will continue until every employee in the company knows the vision and has had the opportunity to provide their thoughts on making it real."

During the last part of the meeting, the goal teams began developing plans to implement the vision. There were five goal teams and each was to develop an effective operating strategy. The teams were Financial Results, Market Position, Customer Relations, Quality of Work Life, and Community Responsibility.

Our survey at Barnett was conducted in May of 1995. Paul Kerins shared the results of that survey with senior management and the affiliates that participated: "We said, 'Are we seeing anything there that is at odds with our Operating Vision, any cause for realignments?' We didn't see anything that jumped out at us. We did see that there was a clear need for more effective communication, there was unevenness."

Paul explained what they planned to do: "We have an annual employee appreciation day, and as a part of that we will put out a report on what the five goal teams have done the previous year. So much of what the goal teams have done is with the Operating Vision in mind. For example, we introduced a scholarship program for employees' children this year. That came directly from the efforts of the quality of work life goal team.

"And our Take Stock in Children program is a major statewide initiative that came from the community responsibility goal team. But we failed to go back to employees and make the connection between these activities and the vision. We've been at a comfort level, because we knew where they came from. But it is clear that the entire employee population isn't seeing that linkage.

"We have just finished redesigning, for the first time, a system-wide approach to new employee orientation. Before, each affiliate handled their own. We now have a curriculum with a heavy emphasis on the vision that every new employee will participate in."

Richard "Rick" Jones, Chief Asset Management Executive, took it back one step further. Rick handles non-banking financial services such as insurance and brokerage: "I came on board fifteen months ago and built a new team. One of the things that attracted me to Barnett was their stated vision and their commitment and the way they want to do business. Our customers like us. I've worked at other financial institutions where customers didn't like us. Why they like Barnett, I think, is the way we have empowered our people, the way we've got people who care and feel good about Barnett.

"So I also use this as a recruiting tool as I bring people into the organization. It helped me select people who would come with a bias toward the company, who cared about its business, but who also cared about its customers and its people."

We asked Rick how he did that: "I ask them to describe how they get things done, what's important to them in how they manage. Plus, I'm a believer that you can assess integrity in an interview if you ask about it. I do pretty aggressive reference checks. We also use a psychologist who's been very helpful."

Paul described what was done to see that the understanding and relevance of the beliefs was taken down level by level rather than everything coming from on high: "The strength of our organization is in our local market autonomy. So you find some people doing that exceptionally well, some not so well. Where it's well done, the vision is prominently displayed in the workplace, every meeting opens with it. If audiovisuals are used, the first is of the vision. People try to relate specifics to it. Is it uniformly done? No. It's a function of the passion and commitment of the local management.

"We are trying to strengthen that by never putting anything up in isolation without referencing back to the vision. As mentioned previously, we now have a system-wide new employee orientation. In the same way we are doing a lot of training on needs-based selling—making sure we are not selling customers products they don't need. This comes directly out of the vision."

We asked Allen how he used the vision in strategic and operational decision making: "For example, one of the statements is that we want to be the nationally recognized standard in the industry. That implies we can't get there by doing everything for everybody. We have to get focused on businesses and products and markets that will achieve both the market and financial return that will put us in that nationally recognized category. It helps us recognize which businesses are mature and won't contribute as much financially. In our business, for publicly held companies, it's EPS growth, among other things, that's the scoreboard. So, I think the vision helps us focus more on those things that will create value for our shareholders.

"We also say we want to make our customers feel like they're home. Banking is a very relationship-oriented business. The trust we develop over time cannot be violated if we are going to maintain our market position. Therefore, it is important to us as we develop products, incentive programs, and operating strategies that the paramount consideration is to take care of our customers—what's in their best interest and ours long term.

"I've thought about how I define my job a number of times. One primary responsibility is to establish the goal—where we want to be. That's helped by the vision—being the nationally recognized standard. Another is to establish the principles that are important to us. Those are represented in the vision. I also balance the needs of our shareholders, customers, and employees in a manner appropriate to the organization and to those constituent groups. Also, we must manage the pace of change so we don't get too far ahead or behind.

"Finally, 'walk the talk.' We created the vision as a team and it is every individual's responsibility to reinforce it in day-to-day interfaces. So, I look for opportunities to get involved in community activities, get involved with employee programs—making sure people are focused on the financial and quantitative objectives of the vision. I spend a good bit of time in the organization in various units talking with people at any level, having lunch, doing branch business, that kind of thing."

Rick commented on what the vision does for his new team: "It provides criteria against which you can judge their actions. My group believes they're in the vanguard of taking Barnett from being a traditional bank to being something that's different. The people that we've brought in want to be a part of something that's positive and forthcoming. The 'we help each other succeed' part of the vision is a way to keep politics out of the decision-making process. If you are focused on dealing with people openly and in a straightforward fashion, it really gives you a set of operating guidelines to have the team succeed beyond the individuals."

Paul comments on what Barnett is doing to measure satisfaction with and application of their beliefs: "The Employee Opinion Survey every two years is primary. We have now built into the survey specific dimensions on the Operating Vision (basic beliefs). Also we just made a major investment to provide 360-degree feedback for every employee in the company. We've done it so far with 1,000 managers. We've bought a technology which is computer assisted and delivered. We use an outside firm to correlate and interpret the results and they go back only to the individual and that is all confidential. Then it is up to the individual to use that information for developmental purposes. Eventually that will cover all 22,000 employees.

"We have five jobs, affecting 8,500 people, where we see the most change because of our Mission and Operating Vision. They include, for example, office manager, teller, and financial consultant. By year-end [1996], we will have finalized what those jobs should look like, and we will put into the system the competencies that should be demonstrated to be successful in that job. Team orientation is absolutely one of the competencies in all the job profiles. Another has to do with customer relations."

Paul continues: "Then an employee can go into one of our employee development centers and do a self-assessment against those profiles. He or she can develop a 360-degree feedback and see how close they come to the critical success factors. Some may be so far off they need to look elsewhere. For others it will say, 'You are all right.' The system will actually draw out a recommended development template to close a particular employee's gaps. To me this is a most powerful thing. I see it coming from line people who say, 'This is what it's going to take to be successful at Barnett in the future.'"

We asked Paul how those who produce an outstanding result from the application of the vision are rewarded: "We've implemented within the last twelve months a spot bonus plan. Among the things we cite are people who are a living example of making the vision real—specifically with reference to customers, community, and financial issues. That is down at the division level. An award up to a maximum of $2,000 can be made. And those are people who would usually not be incentive eligible.

"We do an awful lot of noncash recognition: articles in employee publications where we spotlight people who have gone the extra mile in terms of customer service, helping fellow employees, helping in the community."

Allen sees an important part of his job as getting personally involved in supporting the Operating Vision: "We were working out at the 'Y' the other day and the community development officer informed me that she was in New York to receive an award for Barnett in raising money for the March of Dimes. She mentioned one of our campaign coordinators in the Gainesville community had been recognized nationally as doing the best job as a coordinator. I called her immediately and congratulated her. She did a good job and deserved a personal thank you. Charlie Rice [Charles Rice, Chairman and CEO] will talk to the Board about this, and we will probably do a piece in our employee publication."

Paul comments on the other side—what happens when someone takes an action that really violates the operating vision: "Well, some are more obvious than others. On the customer side, we have changed the way we measure customer service so that it's longer-term, rather than a transactional approach. Clearly, if someone is doing something dysfunctional like selling a customer something they don't need or not being responsive to a customer need and empathetic, there is discipline and in some cases termination. I think the area we are seeing more of this recently is where team players are too motivated by their own objectives exclusive of others. We've said, 'You know, unless you change your behavior, you just don't appear to fit here.'"

We asked Paul if that kind of discipline came from supervision or was motivated within the team: "It's clear that those who are performing well above standard have the strongest sense of team. We have offices where we never have any turnover, because the sense of team becomes so compelling. If someone new comes and isn't flexible enough to help someone who needs time off to take care of a sick child—well, the team just doesn't tolerate that. The person moves on because they are not accepted by the team." We sensed Paul's drive was to make that team spirit uniform system-wide.

Rick comments on how the values in the vision help his team: "I mandate and require openness in issues dealing with each other. This group as a whole bought into the approach to organization development that we've embarked upon. But, sometimes emotions get in the way, particularly in a new team. You just have to get everyone to believe it's important to deal in a straight, open fashion. The issue comes up when the heat of battle or debate surfaces concerns about trust or motive. I've tried to be very sensitive in making sure that people understand each other's motives. I force discussion on what's really happening and what we are trying to do. The initial reaction is, 'I'd rather not do that.' We are going through a thing now—two sales members of my team in competing sales organizations debating who should create the stuff. Feelings came into play. They didn't want to deal openly. Each said to me, 'You tell me what my behavior should be, and I'll modify mine.' But after a couple of sessions they both think openness is a value, and we're redefining our goal and the handoffs and methodology together."

We asked Paul whether they tied reward mechanisms to support team building and results: "Every branch employee, with the exception of the office manager, is part of a team incentive group. We concluded that cash incentive should be team-based among our nonexempt population. We built the incentive as a team. Last year it capped at 8 percent. Next year we're taking the cap off, so it's a pretty compelling message. As far as individual performance, we recognize that in noncash ways."

Paul commented on the ways employees might report a beliefs violation if they were uncomfortable confronting it directly: "We have four primary ways. First, you go through the hierarchy, just like the old grievance procedure. If you're not comfortable with that, we have a corporate ombudsman. The person reports administratively to me, but meets directly with Allen at least once every quarter. Everything is handled in absolute confidence. Then we have a business abuse hotline. Employees have a hard time with that. They see it outside the vision. It appears a bit like telling on your buddy. That system goes through our security department, and we've had very little use of it. Finally, we have on-line access to what is called 'Ask Allen.' Anyone can e-mail him and say, 'Here is something bothering me,' or 'I don't understand this,' or 'Here is a suggestion.' He reads every single one and sees they are handled. He does farm them out for analysis, so he'll give me those having to do with human resources. But Allen will read every answer, occasionally change it, and then send it out."

The results of the 1996 Employee Opinion Survey conducted during April and May showed that there was real progress on parts of the vision and work still required on other parts. There were 16,720 responses covering 84 percent of the employee population. Fifteen dimensions were rated. A rating of 60 percent favorable on any dimension was deemed an organizational strength. Ratings varied from 79 percent to 40 percent favorable.

On the "real progress" side, the dimension on Organization Image received a 79 percent favorable rating, the highest. It dealt with employees' perceptions of issues such as company reputation as an employer, among customers, and within the community. It also covered quality of product and customer service. The dimension Culture: The Work Environment received a 71 percent favorable rating, third highest. It included questions about identifying customer needs and developing products to fit those needs. It also covered employee creativity, quality of work life, and treatment with dignity and respect.

On the "work required" side, dimensions on the Operating Vision and Team Orientation rated just an average 60 percent favorable. The Work Effectiveness dimension scored 40 percent favorable, the lowest. This dimension rated obstacles that prevented employees from being more productive. These obstacles centered around short-term work pressures, policies impacting customer service, uncertainty about job security, and inflexibility and lack of resources. The dimension Sales Orientation (only completed by those involved in direct sales) scored 54 percent favorable, second lowest.

The highly-rated "strength dimensions" suggest that much progress has been made on the Mission and Operating Vision as a way of life at Barnett. The lower-rated "opportunity area dimensions" suggest that this is a never-ending project for any organization. Barnett people are convinced that through their values the mission will be accomplished. Energizing the five goal teams—Financial Results, Market Position, Customer Relations, Quality of Work Life, Community Responsibility—to improve and accelerate the building of those beliefs into plans and actions for their area is the first key. To illustrate, the Quality of Work Life team has developed and put in place a number of major initiatives. They include: Diversity Awareness Training for all employees, Barnett Scholarship Program for children of employees, adoption assistance/leave, Community Family Outreach Program, local employee development centers, casual dress policy.

The ultimate key is for line management, with the help of all the ideas suggested in this case history and their own creativity, to carry these plans and actions into every corner of the organization. The high peaks of nationally recognized standard, improving the lives of customers, improving the well-being of communities, and creating a caring and proud team Barnett can be conquered.

Allen explained how important the vision was to Barnett's future: "I think it's very critical. It provides the principles or defines the behaviors that we want all of our employees to subscribe to and act out. One of the reasons we articulated a statement like that is we hope that the employees, in the thousands of decisions that are made every day, can use that as a frame of reference for any dilemma they face—what course of action is appropriate given what we want to be in the future."

One hundred dollars invested in Barnett Banks, Inc. common stock on December 31, 1990, with all dividends reinvested, was worth $546 on December 31, 1996. Barnett announced on January 15, 1997 that all 22,000 employees (full-, part-, and peak-time) were granted a 200-share stock option at $41 per share. The option can be exercised when the stock hits $66 per share or in five years, whichever comes first.

THE J. M. SMUCKER COMPANY

This is the story of a company that has espoused basic beliefs since its founding in 1897. It is a family-operated business with a fierce pride in its independence. It also has strong beliefs about the quality of its products and its people and the loyalty that it has created in its customer base. Many people don't even know it is publicly traded.

This brief history is from a video Smucker uses for both internal and external presentations: "In 1897, Jerome Smucker opened an apple cider mill, soon joined by apple butter. So basic was his belief in the importance of quality that he hand-signed each crock. With his signature of guarantee, Jerome Smucker always held that you earn a customer's loyalty by providing that customer with a quality product sold at a fair price. Strong ethics, after all, were a major ingredient in the recipe. If that was true for the products, it was true for the whole company. The stewardship of the company name and heritage is that the company remains fully in control of its own destiny. Growth has more to do with overall excellence than overall size."

Not much has changed today about those beliefs. Though they have been adapted to fit modern practices, the intent remains the same:

THE J. M. SMUCKER COMPANY
BASIC BELIEFS

Basic Beliefs are an expression of the Company's values and principles that guide strategic behavior and direction. The Basic Beliefs are deeply rooted in the philosophy and heritage of the Company's founder.

In 1897, The Smucker Company was formed by a dedicated, honest, forward-looking businessman, J. M. Smucker. Because he made a quality product, sold it at a fair price, and followed sound policies, this Company prospered. Today, we who inherit the Smucker name and the Smucker tradition of successful business operations, base present policies on these time-honored principles. We interpret them, in terms of modern corporate thinking, to be the guideposts of our operations. They are as follows:

Quality

Quality applies to our products, our manufacturing methods, our marketing efforts, our people, and our relationships with each other. We will only produce and sell products that enhance the quality of life and well-being. These will be the highest quality products offered in our respective markets because Smucker's growth and business success have been built on quality. We will continuously look for ways to achieve daily improvements that will, over time, result in consistently superior products and performance.

At Smucker's, quality comes first. Sales growth and earnings will follow.

People

We will be fair with our employees and maintain an environment that encourages personal responsibility. In return, we expect our employees to be responsible for not only their individual jobs but for the Company as a whole.

We will seek employees who are committed to preserving and enhancing the values and principles inherent in our Basic Beliefs through their own actions. We firmly believe that:

> Highest quality people produce the highest quality products and service.

> Highest business ethics require the highest personal ethics.

> Responsible people produce exceptional results.

Ethics

The same, strong ethical values on which our Company was founded provide the standard by which we conduct our business as well as ourselves. We accept nothing less regardless of the circumstances. Therefore, we will maintain the highest standards of ethics with our shareholders, customers, suppliers, employees and communities where we work.

Growth

Along with day-to-day operations, we are also concerned with the potential of our Company. Growing is reaching for that potential whether it be in the development of new products and new markets, the discovery of new manufacturing or management techniques, or the personal growth and development of our people and their ideas.

We are committed to a strong balanced growth that will protect or enhance our consumer franchise within prudent financial parameters, thereby providing a fair return for our stockholders on their investment in us.

Independence

We have a strong commitment to stewardship of the Smucker name and heritage. We will remain an independent company because of our desire and motivation to control our own direction and succeed on our own. We strive to be an example of a company which is successful by operating under these Beliefs within the free enterprise system.

These Basic Beliefs regarding quality, people, ethics, growth, and independence have served as a strong foundation in our history. They will continue to be the basis for future strategy, plans, and achievements.

We asked how the basic beliefs were presented. Tim Smucker, Chairman: "They were part of the strategy. There were various elements of the strategy that we covered with different constituents, and the basic beliefs we shared with anybody, internally or externally."

Smucker uses an ethics program as one important way to share its basic beliefs internally. We asked for a description of the ethics program. Tim continues: "I think ethics are easy. It means being truthful, treating your employees like you want to be treated. When we came into association with the Institute of Global Ethics, they had done some thinking on how you can be ethically fit. Their proposition was, 'You need to be aware of what an ethical decision is.' We liked that approach."

The following paraphrases what Bob Ellis, Vice President of Human Resources, said in a phone conversation to provide more detail. Smucker developed their program from one offered by the Institute of Global Ethics, a non-profit, Maine-based organization. The Smucker program is one day in length and mandatory for all employees. Its focus is on Smucker beliefs, not the individuals'.

The first section is a briefing on awareness of ethics. In the second section small break-out groups discuss and come to conclusions on what they see as values or beliefs at Smucker. A full group review generally shows the subgroups have reached similar conclusions—trust, respect, fairness, empathy. The focus of the third section is on ethical decision making.

Handling "right versus wrong" issues is fairly easy. It's tougher coping with "right versus right" ethical decisions. To illustrate simply: There is a broken window and you know a good friend of yours broke it. You have been taught the virtue of honesty, but also the strength of loyalty. This section deals with on-the-job examples and discussion in four areas of "right versus right" choice: short-term/long-term, self/others, justice/mercy, and truth/loyalty. The final section covers rules for ethical decisions: the Golden Rule idea, the greatest good for the greatest number, or a choice that will set a standard. Bob said they have only had two instances in which an employee felt concerned that this program would conflict with or diminish personal values. Both were successfully handled.

Steve Ellcessor, Vice President of Administration, Secretary, and General Counsel, went on to say how the importance of basic beliefs is transmitted down through the organization: "I think the feedback we have gotten is that the development of the ethics program, along with the Smucker Quality Management Program, have been very important in convincing people throughout the organization that the company and the family are serious about basic beliefs."

Bob explains the Quality Management Program. Like the ethics program, it is required for all employees, but it is organized by responsibility level. The plant employee program is two days in length. It provides the skill base to produce Smucker-level quality. It deals with doing it the right way the first time, being responsible for everything around you, putting the same quality level into all actions and relationships. The supervisory program is three days long. It focuses on how to manage quality through teamwork, coaching, and facilitation. The management program covers instilling Smucker quality inside, but also taking the message outside to customers, suppliers, and the investment community.

Richard Smucker, President, cited an example of carrying the beliefs message externally: "We have an analyst who's followed us for the last ten years, really knows the company well. As you know, a financial analyst sometimes looks at just the numbers. He brought in two of his investment bankers with the thought of providing us some service. But before he brought them in, he gave them our beliefs and said whatever solutions they came up with had to be within the parameters of those beliefs. The investment bankers said that really narrowed the choices because they were stringent beliefs."

Both the ethics program and the quality program originated directly from the basic beliefs.

We asked for specific examples of how Smucker top management applied basic beliefs in their decision making. Tim talked about a restructuring program at their Orrville, Ohio plant: "The basic beliefs were the key to how we developed the plan in terms of how we wanted to treat our employees. We referenced the beliefs in the presentation, and we emphasized that we wanted to do something that was right for all the employees. These are not easy decisions, but we have to think of the long term. The people are our company. There has to be an awareness that one of our beliefs says, 'You have to be responsible for everything around you, not just your own individual area.' When you have a tough decision to make, the basic beliefs are the key to implementing it."

Bob described the restructuring situation as basically adding a third shift to the plant. That improved productivity and strengthened all stakeholders for the future. But it also meant that those on the original two shifts gave up considerable overtime compensation and many would be changing jobs. The strength of feeling about basic beliefs helped carry that difficult decision successfully through.

Paul Smucker, Chairman of the Executive Committee, gave another example: "I think a good example of senior management applying basic beliefs, that probably cost the company some money, was when we had to make a decision to sell Elsenham Quality Foods in England. Our main objective was to sell to a company that would keep the plant employees there. So we had to go through a group of different companies that might have bought it. But they didn't meet our requirements, because they were going to close down the plant. It took us more time to sell the operation, but we accomplished our goal. We might have saved money if we'd sold it earlier, but that's the ultimate in following the basic beliefs. We followed the same concept in selling the Smith Pie Company. Actually, that worked out better for the employees. There was progressive growth, because it was sold to a company in the business."

Tim added: "When we purchase any company, we talk about the basic beliefs. We say right up front, we don't expect you to believe these on face value. You challenge them. Do we live them or don't we? Then you have people living what they're preaching."

Steve carries on: "I think that was also reflected in 1995 when we began working on the 'Apple Seed Project.' That involved a large group of our people trying to identify competencies. They spent an awful lot of time and effort trying to understand how the basic beliefs and the people fit in. There was a strong feeling throughout the group that there was something special about the organization, something different about its people. They were trying to figure out if how we hire, train, and manage people was a competency. Ultimately, where I think the group came down was that, no, it's probably not a competency as such. It's just the basic beliefs and it's fundamental."

Bob provides detail on the Apple Seed Project. It was a unique project. Smucker had a couple of flat years—good, but not up to expectations. They worked with an outside firm to do two things.

First, they looked at ways to improve future growth. A 120-member cross-functional, cross-level team reviewed basic beliefs, looked at external trends, and identified competencies. Then they determined what opportunities were out there. Beyond the team, any employee in the company could participate—through their work group, the suggestion box, or an 800 number. From the many ideas generated, twelve new venture areas were selected. Each of those twelve cleared the hurdle—they did not violate any of the basic beliefs. Formal business plans were developed for each venture and suggested priorities were set. The more a venture supported the basic beliefs, the higher its priority. At this writing (late 1996) senior management is reviewing these efforts for next actions. The process still flows from beliefs through strategic intent or architecture, and on to new growth ventures.

As a second part of the project, the same 120-person team, again with input from any employee, looked inside to see what costs could be saved and how quality could be improved. Each operation and job was challenged for change or elimination, always keeping the basic beliefs as the template for recommended actions. From this effort, Smucker has made a pledge to its shareholders of specific dollar savings over a specific time period. Those savings are to be shared with the consumer.

Tim illustrates how the competencies came from the basic beliefs: "Well, two of the competencies—relationships and emotional bonding—really are a direct result of the basic beliefs. Both of those hearken back to the fact that the relationships we developed internally as well as externally were based on the heart and soul of the company, which are the basic beliefs."

Richard takes over the answer: "[The emotional bonding] is how people perceive our brand and our company. We asked the consumer for those things they emotionally bond with at Smucker, and it's a quality product and a quality company. The independence one is that they always think of us not only as an independent company but also as a small, private, family business. So there's that emotional bonding and how we're viewed by the consumer which really relates back to our basic beliefs and the image we portray."

Back to Tim: "It's reinforcing that the outside firm we worked with on Apple Seed had ten different partners with extensive knowledge of other companies. They kept bouncing our beliefs back to us. We felt that emotional bonding and relationships sound like motherhood and apple pie. We're so close to it. But they kept replaying, 'This is unique.' They hadn't seen this to this extent elsewhere, and it wasn't coming top-down. We had 120 people from the shop floor and throughout the whole organization saying it over and over again."

Steve adds, "The beliefs permeated the discussion. It's not that people sat down and said, 'This belief means this and that belief means that.' They were the underlying assumptions upon which all of the discussions were based."

We asked about the impact of basic beliefs in hiring and promotion decisions. Tim comments: "We do have a pretty extensive interview process. You have to have people who understand it before they come to the organization. We're not instilling the values in these people—they are coming to the company with them. The only thing we do is determine whether they have them or not."

Steve adds to this point: "During the Apple Seed Project, our team talked with lots of outsiders including recruiters who have done work with us over the years. Uniformly, those folks came back saying that we were one of the most difficult companies to work for in hiring people. We want to look at a lot of people, we're choosy about the people we look at, and we have more people at higher levels interviewing these folks than most other companies."

Paul speaks about promotions and beliefs: "As far as promotions, people who have responsibility and authority within the company have to demonstrate the beliefs without shouting it from the rooftops, without a tag on your coat. That's what we're trying to do. I feel confident that we've demonstrated it with those who have responsibility and that's now beginning to sift down to different levels of management throughout the organization."

We received a very thought-provoking response when we asked how people were rewarded and recognized down the line for exemplary application of the beliefs. Tim and Richard commented: "When we looked at your survey results, we noted that there was not a feeling that employees who practiced the beliefs were rewarded and recognized. As far as reward, I'm not sure there should be. I think it should be a part of their everyday jobs. I mean, it's an expectation—if someone is supposed to be honest, do you reward him for the fact that he is honest? That's what makes us unique. The reward is being part of an

organization that lives by its principles. That's the reward."
Steve adds: "As far as recognition, clearly their manager should
recognize and appreciate it, make it known. But that's part of
being a good manager."

Conversely, we asked, what should be done about a violation of beliefs? Richard, Tim, and Steve all comment: "Depends on what the violation is. If it's a misunderstanding, it's
just good management to counsel and work with the person. If
it's a flagrant violation, like theft, there's no second chance.
Putting our quality in jeopardy in any way: there are certain
things that are not acceptable. This would be very rare. But, on
occasions, we have had to dismiss people for just cause."

We asked about the relationship of the beliefs to the bottom
line. Tim responds: "I think there is a direct relationship. We
don't talk to outside people on a frequent basis because they
can't really understand what the company's about and the fact
that we do understand. If we put the beliefs first, the results
will be there—both top and bottom line. Our belief about
growth is entrenched in the concept that as ideas grow, so do
people grow. We are not interested in growth that will take us
up huge one year and then down the next year. We want steady,
continual growth. So that's a concept of growth we think is
unique. It does limit us from getting into fad-type products that
may not be in sync with the beliefs, but could bring us short-
term sales and profit gains.

"The people belief, 'being responsible for everything around
you—you see something and you do something about it,' ties to
the bottom line. You have your peripheral vision out, and if
you're an accounting person and you see something you can
bring to a marketing person, that should be a natural part of
your job. You have more open thinking and have a responsibility for the results of the company as a whole. There is a real relationship between the basic beliefs and longer-term shareholder value."

Even with all of this emphasis on beliefs, our survey did
show a diminution in terms of the recognition of the importance of the beliefs as we went down several levels in the orga-

nization. Richard addressed that issue: "We only implemented our Smucker Quality Management Program and our Ethics Program in the last few years. They include our training package on basic beliefs. So, even though we lived it and communicated it, our formal training down at the hourly level has only been in the last few years. At management levels we have been doing this training for fifteen years. That's probably one of the reasons you saw that."

Even for a company like Smucker that has worked so hard to make beliefs a way of life, the above illustrates there is always more that can be done. Beliefs need fine-tuning. Tim says: "You put them down and you have to live them, but also if you really understand you have to expand on them. Over the years we've been very careful to add nuances that make them more meaningful, more understandable." Powerful new ways to build beliefs, as the ethics and quality programs do, must be developed and continually improved. Finding ways to live the beliefs so that the true reward for their application is being a part of that organization is challenging and exciting.

Certainly Smucker has some advantages in living its beliefs, because the Smucker family is leading the charge. An employee puts it this way: "We have pride in the Smucker name and the reputation we have. I think we take pride in that we've been able to maintain that independence. We are the Smucker company. We're not some part of something else—some big conglomerate back in New York, Boston, or Philadelphia. We're small, we're tough, we're good."

Smucker beliefs are so deeply ingrained that I think the company will continue to grow and prosper in the years ahead, and, perish the thought, even if they run out of Smuckers. I also think most any organization—if they care, if they see the connection between basic beliefs and long-term sustained success, and if they work at it—can take the Smucker message and the messages from our other three companies and improve their basic beliefs processes.

One hundred dollars invested in J. M. Smucker Company common stock in 1979, the year they committed their beliefs to writing, with all dividends reinvested, would be worth $2,466 in 1996. The number of employees grew from 1,236 to 1,927 over the same period.

These four chapters have demonstrated the dedication and effort it takes to put basic beliefs to work. The four companies, and the others discussed in Chap. 2, see the positive results but are ever diligent in improving their basic beliefs processes. It's an imperfect world—things can go wrong.

In the next chapter we explore pitfalls or roadblocks that can detour the benefits of basic beliefs.

PITFALLS ALONG
THE WAY

Pitfalls are problems that interfere with an effective basic beliefs process. When one surfaces it needs quick recognition and correction. Hopefully this chapter will reduce these pitfalls to potential problems that can be anticipated and prevented. Basic beliefs guide decision making; the basic beliefs process makes sure that happens. But things can go wrong.

FAILURE TO WALK THE TALK

While this is a common excuse for all sorts of business problems, if it happens there is no chance to reap the rewards of a fully functioning basic beliefs process. Top management may set clear and specific basic beliefs, but if what they do ignores or conflicts with those beliefs, that is the reality. That is also true if they condone behavior by others that violates those beliefs.

Gary Edwards of the Ethics Research Center offers an extreme observation: "'Much bad conduct results from people taking decisions they know absolutely are wrong. They act in the belief that certain actions are expected by supervisors or senior management even if the actions violate stated policy.'

"The heat is on to generate the numbers, ship product out the door, produce the profit. 'People decide to get the numbers in and the pressure builds up to lie, cheat and steal,' says Edwards." And further in the same article: "Still, there seems little doubt that for all the talk about 'changing the culture,' ethics programs can have only a limited influence on corporate wrongdoing. In one survey of top executives, 60% thought unethical conduct and illegal behavior in business had increased. But far more said the solution lay more in effective leadership by corporate chieftains than in voluntary compliance and self-policing."[1]

When senior leadership doesn't follow through, the negative results can be far-reaching. Remember the Exxon Valdez oil spill: "Rawl [CEO] says he didn't go to Alaska at once because the cleanup was in capable hands and he had 'many other things to do.' ... By going to Alaska and acquitting himself well in the spotlight, Rawl would have accomplished two purposes: He would have reassured the public that the people who run Exxon acknowledged their misdeed and would make amends. And he might have salvaged the pride that Exxon workers once had in their company. Says one manager: 'Whenever I travel now, I feel like I have a target painted on my chest.' Employees are confused, embarrassed, and betrayed. Says an executive working in New Jersey: 'The company is in turmoil. It's hard to get decisions.'"[2]

John W. Teets, former Chairman and CEO of the Dial Corporation, apparently does not see or agree with "walk the talk" on basic beliefs: "... when he moved to close six consumer-products plants and eliminate 700 jobs, Mr. Teets has built a reputation as a man with an iron grip on company costs. He has even set up an 'asset protection program' to make sure that expenses are not padded by improper employee use of company resources. That is the clear message from Mr. Teets' office: cut costs, live sparingly, and never, ever, treat the company's assets as your own." The article continues on to show the contrasts: board approval of $10 million in company money to invest in a major league baseball franchise in which Teets is a general partner; compensation of $8.5 million, far higher than other CEOs in the industry; corporate jets and a nine-member aviation department; a company-owned apartment on Central Park South in Manhattan; and, of course, nine of eleven directors recruited by Mr. Teets.[3] What does this imply as far as beliefs about quality, hard work, trust, and productivity with those down the line who make the Dial Soap, Breck Shampoo, and Brillo Pads?

Not only must the CEO practice what he or she preaches, but it's also important to maintain relationships down through the organization. Consultant Richard Hagberg has some gloomy news in this regard based on a database of characteristics of 511 CEOs: "Under the stress and pressure that go with the job, many CEOs become reactive, listen less, and act impulsively without thinking. Their impatience drives them to focus on financial goals, which means they fail to build relationships with boards or their employees.... As they distance themselves from others, it becomes harder for people to disagree with them. When that happens, they stop getting bad news or the benefit of a give-and-take conversation.... Teamwork, which you need in any corporation, suffers." It's going to be tough to make basic beliefs work if that happens. But the article goes on to provide some hope: "But CEOs didn't get where they are by being stupid. If given credible feedback, they frequently run with it."[4]

What is recognized and rewarded ultimately determines behavior and performance. If that is in conflict with a stated belief, then just bury the belief—it's dead anyway: "Less blatant but no less fatal are the cynicism and resentments that build when management preaches one doctrine and practices another.... They preach the importance of teamwork—then reward individuals who work at standing out from the crowd. They announce a preference for workers with broad experience—then denounce job jumpers within the organization. They encourage risk taking—then punish good-faith failures. Says [Arthur D. Little's] Scott Morgan: 'It really is tantamount to managerial malpractice.'"[5]

We asked our respondents this question:

"To what extent do you find yourself in situations where you are expected to do something counter to the company's stated basic beliefs?"

Possible answers were:

Not at All	Limited Extent	Moderate Extent	Considerable Extent	Great Extent
1	2	3	4	5

The average from all four companies was 2.0 with a range from 1.7 to 2.1.

It is probably unrealistic to think there will ever be an average response of "1—Not at All." Certainly the benefits of adhering to the basic beliefs should be known. But the real world will never be perfect. Perhaps these selected quotes from our final survey question, "Any other comments?" might shed some light on that imperfect world and why the average was not closer to 1.

- "I think when the product is the wrong size something should be done. Sometimes the supervisor just says run it."

- "It seems that sometimes we are not providing the best possible product. There is a lot of pressure of not having downtime. If we took ten minutes to fix the problem, we would produce a better-looking product."

- "In a conflict between political considerations and the company's basic beliefs, politics usually wins most of the time."

- "We reward and promote those who get it done. The 'how' appears irrelevant."

- "There is so much pressure on sales ... To meet your sales goals each month you sometimes don't do what is best for the customer."

- "Day-to-day business decisions are still being driven by profitability and budget and not by basic beliefs."

An effective beliefs process should turn some of these situations around. Let me also add that there were many more positive than negative responses to this question.

These quotes do no imply that the answer is to lower cost, production, sales, and profitability goals and raise budgets to follow beliefs. But those goals should be set with these questions in mind:

- Is this goal pushed so hard that a basic belief is or could be compromised?

  Sales output versus customer service

  Product quantity versus quality

  Cost versus efficient and preventive maintenance

- Is this goal set at such an unreasonably high level that ignoring or violating basics beliefs is virtually required to accomplish it?

  Sales quotas

  Cost or budget constraints

  Timing deadlines

- Is the accomplishment of this goal so rewarding in the short term that a basic belief protecting longer-term sustained growth and reputation could be violated?

  Sales commission/bonus schemes that lead to overselling, phony bookings, customer fleecing

  Offshore cost advantages leading to bribes, kickbacks, use of child labor

  Marketing pressures that lead to false advertising, uneven pricing, under-the-table deals

Under-the-table deals for the cause of self-interest do not model basic beliefs: "Early in December, *Smart Money*'s editor-at-large James J. Cramer, 40, wrote an article for his monthly column, *Unconventional Wisdom*, recommending four $2 to $6 'orphan' stocks. During December—before the article was published in the February issue—Cramer's money management firm ... spent more than $1 million acquiring roughly 280,000 shares of at least 3 of the stocks. When the magazine finally reached its 550,000 regular readers in mid-January, prices of the normally thinly traded issues surged 18% to 100% in a matter of days. Trading records show that at the peak, Cramer's firm had paper profits of more than $2 million on the stocks."[6]

I don't know much about financial publishing; but having been in a professional business and as a user of financial newsletters, that behavior strikes me as being completely unethical. The article from *Money* magazine goes on to say that Cramer's boss—*The Wall Street Journal*—defended the action. *Smart Money*'s editor says it's in his contract to do this. It may not be illegal, but it certainly undermines the trust of the magazine's readers.

The article goes on to say how *Money* magazine handles financial publishing. "We take our responsibility so seriously at *Money* that we captured it in a credo mounted on the wall where everyone can see it: OUR READERS ABOVE ALL. In addition, like virtually every other financial publication, we enforce a written conflict-of-interest policy. We explicitly prohibit staffers as well as 'anyone connected with' us, including outside writers, from trading in securities we are writing about until two weeks after the article goes on sale. We don't set different ethical standards for different writers. How would a double standard serve our readers? They put their trust in everything we choose to publish.

"What if someone tried to skirt our rules? Let me be clear: If the violation was flagrant and willful, I would fire the writer, dismiss any editor who knew about it but did not stop it, and then call in securities regulators to determine whether a crime had occurred."[7]

Arthur D. Little's Chairman, John Magee, provides an apt summary for this pitfall as he reports on their interviews with CEOs of large international companies: "First, the chief executive must be actively and visibly committed to acceptance of high ethical standards throughout the company. This takes work.... Lead by example. The notion 'Do as I say, not as I do' does not apply. One chief executive has given up accepting invitations to golf tournaments and weekends in hunting lodges from customers, suppliers, and business associates.

"Lead in articulating corporate values. A number of respondents describe their personal roles in drafting corporate mission and value statements and testing and refining these through dozens of meetings with staff at all levels around the world. This process has to be repeated perhaps every two or three years."[8]

This is a critical pitfall to address. No matter how sound or well-communicated, credibility and motivation to apply beliefs go out the window when leaders don't practice what they preach. What to do?

- The basic beliefs process must be so ingrained and visible it is tough not to follow it.

- For most of us our conscience tells us in advance when we are about to stray from a belief. Listen to it!

- Be true enough to yourself to assess why you are about to or don't follow a belief. If you feel the intent of a belief needs changing, try to make that happen. If you really don't believe in the beliefs, get out!

- Ask a colleague you respect to keep track of and audit how well you "walk the talk."

- If someone senior to you is not following the beliefs, find reasonable ways to bring that to attention.

- Do not condone failure to follow beliefs in your sphere of responsibility.

MERGERS BRING BELIEFS CONFLICT

Merger mania is here. There are many reasons. For some, mergers seem an easier or faster way to grow and impress the investment community. Some acquire to gain a competitive advantage. Some merge to consciously diversify, reduce costs, or fill a niche in the market. In any case, the goal is always to make one plus one equal three or four or five. But often there is a struggle to make one plus one equal two, and it creates headaches for both parties. We all know of horror stories, mergers that never even made "two" and eventually fell apart, usually with financial loss and a lot of soul-searching. Often the real cause is not a strategic or operational mismatch but incompatible beliefs. Typically product and market factors and the capabilities that support them are thoroughly researched. Financial potential glows. But no one looks at the beliefs of each company to see if they are supportive, slightly different, or incompatible. If any differences are noticed, they are easy to brush off in light of the economic pluses and the excitement of the time.

Northwest Airlines and KLM yield $200 million a year in operating profit from their alliance. Differing beliefs, towering egos, and quests for power may tear it all apart. "The conflict pits Checchi and Wilson [Northwest Cochairmen], two high-flying financial guys, against a bunch of stubborn airline burghers from KLM. The motives are basic: Both sides think they know best how to run an airline, and want to call the shots.... 'This relationship is dysfunctional,' complains Wilson. The top brass from the two carriers don't even talk.... In part, the fight is a classic clash in cultures, a collision of two diametrically opposed philosophies of doing business.... 'It's the European vs. the American way,' says Bouw [Peter Bouw, KLM President].... The Dutch are bluff, unpretentious types who collect modest salaries and disdain glitz. The stocky, ruddy-faced Bouw is a company lifer who unwinds by rowing a shell on the canals near Amsterdam.... Checchi, 48, and Wilson, 56, live like California royalty.... Checchi and Wilson paint the folks at KLM ... as plodding bureaucrats envious of the millions Northwest's managers have earned on surging stock. 'That's laughable,' retorts Bouw. 'We're not jealous. We just appreciate our own values.' For his part Bouw sees Checchi and Wilson as financial carpetbaggers.... 'There is definitely a culture clash,' admits Bouw. 'It hurts in my heart to hear Northwest say the trust is gone.' Though Bouw swears he'd like to continue the union, he recognizes that the bruised feelings may make that impossible."[9]

Such divergent beliefs about lifestyles must have been visible at the get-acquainted stage that led to the relationship. Open and honest discussion of those differences in beliefs could have produced guidelines to manage and control them as they affected key decision making. If that seemed impossible and too disruptive, perhaps discussion should have ceased and different partners considered.

United Airlines and USAir handled their merger discussions better. Gerald Greenwald, CEO, UAL, Inc., says: "I think we gained a lot of insight into employee attitudes, which would have been crucial if we had done the merger. The way these mergers usually work, you take your five or six top people and lock them up in a hotel room with the other guy's five or six top people. Then you go to your boards and eventually you wrap up the deal. You take up issues that involve employees later.

"Instead, we dealt with everything publicly. We talked to our employees on CompuServe, and anybody could have listened in. We were very open about the criteria we wanted to measure, and we wanted to gauge how employees at both United and USAir would respond to the merger. These were fundamental issues. Our people, for example, helped convince us that we would be better off just as we were. And we couldn't have figured all this out without getting plenty of input from our employees."[10]

The merger or "swallowing up" of Chase Manhattan Corporation by the Chemical Banking Corporation brought an end to a basic beliefs heritage at Chase. Downsizing will continue and expand: 12,000 jobs have been eliminated, 100 branches closed. "Like many organizations, Chase is a workplace in transition, a company in which old certainties about work no longer apply.... Indeed, many profoundly depressed Chase employees interpret the deal as a sellout by senior management, the death of the company they cherished." The *New York Times* article devotes considerable coverage to the extensive help given to those leaving. It would seem more effort is devoted to those fired than to those who will remain. While quite a number of younger workers express optimism about the merger, the tone of the article suggests the following represents the feelings of many who, for now, stay. "Of Chase's 126 lawyers, 38 were told that their Chase careers were over. Chemical dismissed 15 of its 150 lawyers.... To the survivors, the place seemed suddenly cold. People felt remorse for those who hadn't made it. A biting joke made the rounds: 'The good news is you have a job. The bad news is you have a job.' The lawyers found ... the Chase determination to be the 'employer of choice' all so irrelevant now."[11]

Senior management of the merged companies must get the word out to the remaining 62,000 employees about the long-term benefits of the merger beyond downsizing. If the beliefs of the merged companies are brought together and reconciled, the new organization has a powerful instrument for handling the short-term duress and improving the long-term stability and growth and potential for new jobs. Beliefs about people and job security must be reinterpreted to mean that employees who have the most up-to-date skills will be employable. Responsibility for that future employment will rest more on the individual. Anxious employees need to know that the merged organization will have beliefs and practices to make it strong and will again become a company in which to have pride.

No one expects honesty, trust, and first-class personal service more than customers dealing with those who handle their money. In his bank-buying binge, Fleet Bank's Chairman and CEO, Terrence Murray, needs to rethink those kinds of beliefs. "He readily says that he aims for B retail service to customers instead of A service because A service is too expensive." Fleet also has been dogged by recurrent snafus and scandals—overcharging second-mortgage borrowers, which provoked a lawsuit and a *60 Minutes* exposé. "Customers had to endure such ills as rapid turnover of account officers, processing errors, and ever changing administrative procedures. Some clients took their business to other institutions. 'Fleet is in the business of buying banks, not in the banking business,' complains Raymond J. Kinley Jr. of Clough Harbour & Associates in Albany, N.Y., a consulting engineering firm that pulled its loan business away from Fleet in 1993."[12] At least for Kinley, that was more D or F service than B.

Seizing the brass ring and acquiring others, rather than being acquired, is certainly a viable business strategy. But if beliefs have not been considered, particularly as they affect employees and customers, the new structure may be a house of cards.

In addressing this pitfall, Jack Welch, CEO of General Electric, has some good advice: "One of the things people don't really understand is that having the company you work for acquired is probably the worst thing that can happen to somebody, other than the loss of a family member. All the things you have learned, all the truths you have known—your boss, where you get your paycheck from, your security—change in one day. New people come in, they talk about their values. At GE, when we've been the acquirer, I don't think we've been as sensitive as we could have been over the years. But in most cases we went too slow in trying to get the new company to adapt to our ways. You know: Let's not give our culture to these people; let's let them be themselves. That's the lesson: You've got to take the actions, get it done, and get on with the game."[13]

Howard Schultz, CEO of Starbucks Coffee Company: "... Starbucks made an $11 million investment in Noah's New York Bagels, a San Francisco-area retailer. Schultz says that for every alliance, there are many more opportunities that are not pursued. 'These are case-by-case decisions with one very specific common thread: the value system of the company in question,' he says. 'We are trying not to align ourselves with a brand or corporation, but with people who view business as we do. One customer at a time, with products that have authenticity and are sustainable. We are not interested in diluting the integrity of Starbucks by creating short-term wins. We aim to create long-term value for both our shareholders and our people."[14]

Last, a quote about Manugistics, Inc.: "A major test of the Manugistics' commitment to its Elements of Excellence [basic beliefs] came with the acquisition of a former competitor at the beginning of 1990.... Even before the merger took place, the human resources department was on-site, not only communicating the Elements of Excellence, but also identifying employees' concerns and questions. To underline the team values of Manugistics, a committee of employees from both organizations worked to develop a logo [EnRoute to the Future] that depicted the strengths of both companies.... At a celebration of the merger ... each employee of the acquired firm was matched with an employee from Manugistics, so that he or she could ask questions about the new company and would know at least one person in the new organization.

"Understanding the anxiety that can exist in this type of situation, the human resources department gave presentations to employees on the new benefits plans and on the value of the merger the day after it was complete. Questions that couldn't be answered by the human resources department were passed on immediately to management, and answers were provided as quickly as possible.

"To help communicate Manugistics' cultural values to employees in the acquired firm, training on active listening and client sensitivity was given to these new employees, and an abbreviated management development class was held within 60 days of the merger. In keeping with the organization's commitment to its partnership with clients [customers] Manugistics closely communicated with its clients throughout the entire merger process. This was particularly important for the companies that had been clients of the acquired firm.

"All of these actions required Herculean efforts on both sides. Through the entire merger process, the Elements of Excellence became the common language to link the two organizations. Employees and managers from both firms took it as a challenge to maintain these values even in the most difficult of situations.

"In looking back, this merger–integration strategy may have cost Manugistics additional time and effort, but it proved to be prudent because it enabled the company to retain the key talent in the acquired firm, help minimize the disruption of both firms' operations, and built the goodwill and trust that were essential."[15]

Basic beliefs are a critical factor for a long-term, successful merger or acquisition. Yet they may often be overlooked. They should be consciously discussed as part of the many feasibility studies leading to the decision. How they impact strategic decisions and day-to-day activities down through each organization should be well sampled. In that way their real intent becomes visible. Too many major differences in beliefs will outweigh a lot of economic and competitive benefits. Smaller differences in beliefs should be ironed out and built into a common statement. When two cultures merge, all employees need to know how to act. Apply a depth of thinking and care that makes beliefs an important part of any merger discussion and decision. Integrating the beliefs of the two companies is the ideal way to bring their cultures together.

OVERRELIANCE ON ETHICS POSITIONS

Dow Corning had an extensive ethics audit process controlled by a significant business ethics executive. All of that didn't prevent the breast implant problem, because that problem was thought to be a business problem and not a moral issue. It's analogous to thinking that a vice president of strategic planning will assure sound strategies or a human resource function will result in effective human relations. Without careful thought, the deceptiveness of these titles leads some to think that the person who has them is the only one responsible for what the name in the title suggests. Ethics managers don't "do" ethics. Ethics managers should support top management in seeing that an effective basic beliefs process is in place, that it is defined, executed, monitored, and evaluated by all those in the organization who live by it and make it work. Throughout this book various responsibilities for an ethics (basic beliefs) function are presented.

If the organization sees the ethics manager as responsible for ethics, then that function becomes just an input to either consider or not as decisions are made. That's apparently what happened at Dow Corning, and the ethics function's input was not considered. That is not good enough. If the role is seen that way, get rid of the role or change it to what it should be. I also favor changing the title from ethics to basic beliefs, because ethics does not fully represent basic beliefs.

Ethics officers and committees should have broad participation from various functions and levels within the organization. Then belief issues are debated and resolved with differing points of view. "Unfortunately, the profile of the typical ethics committee is strongly oriented toward upper management, and designed without much input or representation from lower level employees. Only 23 percent of the Center for Business Ethics survey respondents had managers below the level of the board or executive officers as members of their ethics committees, and only 8 percent had non-managers as members."[16]

While it is important that corporate officers be a part of any basic beliefs committee, they should not be the sole members. If they are, as they work their way through the basic beliefs process their deliberations may be too one-sided or insular. Having a cross-level and cross-function make-up should address this concern. This broad representation should also help facilitate building the basic beliefs process into every level and function in the organization. That's the goal.

ORGANIZATIONAL AND PERSONAL BELIEFS DIFFER

This certainly can happen when organizational beliefs are fuzzy, extreme, or frequently ignored or violated. This can also occur because the way work is performed is changing. More employees work at home. Networking, e-mail, teleconferencing, beepers, faxing, and the like depersonalize work, making supervision and shared beliefs more difficult. Temporary or part-time employees may not buy in to longer-term company beliefs. Decentralization and empowerment give individuals and work teams more responsibility, not only for their work, but for their beliefs. Family values increasingly enter the workplace. Outsourcing puts others' values where yours used to be. Anxious employees, worried about their jobs, may let personal beliefs take over for corporate ones they no longer respect.

Change, which requires new direction and practice, often brings personal beliefs that differ from the organization's to the surface. At K-T, I can recall two such situations. In the early days, our employees did all the instruction in problem solving and decision making for our clients. This limited our growth. In addition, our bigger clients felt this approach was too slow to produce the results they wanted. We had beliefs about growth, that these problem-solving ideas were good for anyone, that the clients should apply the processes themselves, and that the ideas produced practical results. That led us to think about licensing—a client organization could do its own instruction using our ideas. We would train and certify leaders within a client company, and provide materials and ongoing service.

Well, feelings came out fast: They can't possibly do it as well as we can; Our quality will go down; We will lose control; This will be the end of the company. Some felt we were a discipleship—a small, tight, dedicated band of high-quality professional educators creating "born-again" managerial problem solvers and decision makers in our client companies. Some had joined the company because their personal beliefs so strongly supported this idea. I will admit that to some extent we all had that feeling, and it was a good one.

But those in charge felt the licensing approach would greatly expand the application of our ideas as well as the growth of the business and would achieve better results. We made that decision and licensing became a driver of our growth and reputation.

A second potential decision was to take our ideas outside the U.S. That supported our beliefs about growth, that the ideas were important for improving communication and understanding across national boundaries, and enhanced our leadership in process facilitation. Again, there were deep concerns within our small group: We have all the business we can handle in the U.S.; Why take dollars we would make in profit-sharing and invest them overseas; Overseas operations will be impossible to control. Based on our beliefs, we made the decision to go ahead. The plus was that overseas business balanced the ups and downs in the U.S. economy and supported our work with large multinational clients. Today, 50 percent of K-T's business is outside the U.S. The minus was that, even with all our focus on beliefs, there remained some friction between U.S. and foreign operations depending on who was up and who was down. Some K-Ters who had strong feelings against the idea saw the benefits and joined in. Others never did and left the company. That was good both for the organization and for them.

Go with those decisions that are driven by basic beliefs and make economic sense for the long term. Those whose personal beliefs and feelings about those decisions differ in the extreme have to modify their feelings and rejoin the team, or leave.

Each person in a company has many affiliations: company, work unit, profession, union, peers, age group, ethnic group, gender, function, friends, family, etc. Any of these may involve beliefs that surface depending on the situation. Companies should recognize that this diversity can be turned to a competitive advantage. Fully accomplishing that requires rethinking corporate beliefs and their intent. Corporate beliefs must be an umbrella under which relationships and activities that relate to diversity can thrive.

For example, as a *Business Week* supplement pointed out about accomplishing goals: "Organizations are more successful in uniting different groups in the pursuit of common goals when individuals feel secure that their differences are valued."

On ways of accomplishing work: "Effective team performance requires trust and open communication among team members. Employees' understanding and valuing each others' differences is seen as the key to trust and effective communication. Unmanaged diversity can undercut trust, sabotage communication and create barriers to employees and teams achieving their potential."

And on the role of management: "Managers are becoming responsible for working in new ways, from directive to facilitative, to coach and counselor, to empowerer. They are charged with creating effective teams of employees who are unlike themselves in gender, race, religion, culture, language, education, values, lifestyle and family relationships. In total quality management, effectively managing a diverse work force becomes an integral part of enabling employees to perform to their potential."[17]

In each of these areas all employees must know they can apply their own beliefs within the scope and intent of corporate beliefs. They also must know that in a situation where corporate and personal beliefs conflict, and performance will be affected, that should be thought through and addressed.

Corporate beliefs that relate to diversity and the decisions they impact are important factors in future business success. They must be central to the extensive employee and management training required to obtain a competitive advantage from diversity. If diversity programs and training are being considered, plan and do it right: "Companies rarely pursue diversity strategies with the same urgency and commitment as corporate initiatives viewed as directly affecting the bottom line. All too often, squeezed by budget or time constraints, diversity experts' ambitious reforms are reduced to token efforts. A department head rushes through a canned speech for distracted employees. Workers watch an off-the-shelf video. No wonder nothing happens.

"For the programs to work, training and education must be extensive and coupled with vigorous CEO-backed efforts to measure change, hold managers accountable for their implementation, and reward practitioners through compensation.... [W]ithout the institutional framework, urgency, and commitment, diversity training is a prodigious waste of time and money."[18]

Human behavior is complex when it comes to fundamental beliefs or values. There are the basic beliefs of the corporation. There are personal values brought from one's own upbringing and background. There are the values espoused or implied by various diverse affiliations. All of these influence one's decision making, actions, and relationships at work. The wise corporation will think about the decisions, activities, and relationships this diversity should influence and how to maintain the intent of corporate beliefs.

Industry Week asked its readers to contrast and compare what they personally value versus their perception of what is valued by their corporate employers. Here are a few conclusions:

- Approaches that motivate by caring rather than current approaches based on fear
- Approaches that place more value on learning through failure rather than the more common practice of penalizing failure
- More emphasis on the long-term versus American organization cultures which still place moderately more focus on the short-term
- More openness and candor in day-to-day work life versus practices in place that promote secrecy [said by industrial managers]
- A work climate that encourages expression of feelings rather than the current practice which is keep your feelings to yourself
- On-job motivation from personal satisfaction rather than the organization's financial motivation
- Individual efforts motivated by desire to grow and create rather than the organization's tendency to motivate through its own "survival needs"
- More risk taking versus the work environment encouragement to play it safe
- More team and less adversarial thinking[19]

Perceptions such as these need to be considered to reinterpret how beliefs influence decisions in the areas involved.

One way to see that personal and organizational beliefs don't clash is to select and promote those employees whose personal beliefs are in tune with the organization's beliefs. Develop ways to determine and test for this agreement, or lack of same, in initial employment screening. Searching for these beliefs is a part of the interview process, past work experience, and personal reference checks. Knowing whether beliefs match is important for both the organization and the individual: "The savings bank is implementing its cultural values by administering a test instrument to prospective and existing employees that ascertains the degree to which their attitudes are consistent with desired behaviors. Hiring decisions are influenced by the results. Current employees who exhibit the cultural value profile are encouraged and given greater opportunities; those who do not are trained to develop those values. This cultural value profile has been added to the bank's annual performance review, further focusing everyone's attention on key desired behaviors."[20]

Research by Posner and Schmidt lends strong support to this approach. Their conclusions were based on surveys of 6,000 managers from top management to supervisory level. Questions were asked about organizational and personal beliefs: "Managers who felt clear (consonant) about their personal values and organizational values reported positive attitudes about their work and the ethical practices of their colleagues and firms. And managers who experienced contention (ambiguity or lack of clarity) about both their personal and organizational values reported comparably unfavorable work attitudes and beliefs about the ethical practices of their colleagues and firms."[21]

Stephan Covey (author of *Seven Habits of Successful People* and head of the Covey Learning Center) works on this challenge from the individual side: "What Covey teaches is this: To do well you must do good, and to do good you must first be good.... Covey proposes that moral behavior is based on obedience to universal natural laws, or principles, that are immutable. These include, for example, fairness, integrity, honesty, human dignity, service, quality, and excellence." Covey says of his training: "There is nothing new in all this, ... I just built a bridge between the theory and the practice.... We believe that organizational behavior is individual behavior collectivized."[22] I suggest that there is an additional bridge—making sure that those individual behaviors are in sync with and support corporate beliefs.

Discussing personal beliefs is not always easy: "In order to cultivate personal goal-setting in a principle-based climate, it stands to reason that personal principles—you can't do the right thing without first defining 'right'—become matters of public discussion. It is a discussion, Mr. Melrose [Toro CEO] agrees, that not everyone is comfortable with having at work. There were some people who said, 'I'm going to do my job, I'm going to do it well. I'm going to get paid. I'm going to contribute to the team and work toward the mission ... but don't tamper with my values.'"[23]

If any employee wants privacy regarding personal beliefs, that should be his or her choice. And that's okay, as long as work performance incorporates and supports the organization's beliefs. It seems reasonable that as one achieves increasing responsibility in the chain of command, congruence of personal and corporate beliefs becomes more essential. At senior levels, evidence that personal values are negatively influencing decision making suggests an early exit. When organizational and personal beliefs conflict, excellence is difficult to achieve or maintain. When making a decision or engaging in an activity, every employee must know how to think through any such conflict. That means the best possible choice is one that balances those beliefs so as to accomplish the company's purpose and live with oneself.

MULTINATIONAL BUSINESS BLURS BELIEFS

Geographical distance and differing cultural beliefs and practices by region or by country make it difficult to apply corporate beliefs uniformly. These cultural practices make uniform corporate beliefs difficult to apply:

- controlled market entry
- conscious discrimination
- lack of pollution standards
- copyright/patent infringement
- insistence on kickbacks, personal favors
- exploitation of child labor
- unclear legal systems
- systems of government that promote other beliefs
- easy government intervention
- autocratic/authoritative business leadership

The first thing for a company to decide is that its beliefs are powerful enough for long-term success, that they will apply wherever strategic and operational objectives lead. Then it is a matter of knowing the culture and business practices of the country you are considering and determining which beliefs could be compromised by what you plan to do. Decide how those decisions might be executed and controlled so they will not violate beliefs. If that is not feasible, decide not to operate there. Finally, if you make the move, set up monitoring systems to detect what you may have missed, and fix it before it becomes a mess.

Organizations that know and follow their beliefs look first to countries that support those beliefs. But when economic objectives lead a corporation to operate in a country with differing beliefs, they find ways to do business and still stay true to their beliefs.

Arthur D. Little, in a series of conversations with CEOs of large international companies, draws this conclusion: "Is it true that standards of business ethics differ from culture to culture, and that successful multinational companies have to be flexible and do business the local way? We pressed our respondents on this issue and got a unanimous response: No. In fact, they went further: not only is it not necessary or even desirable to compromise on fundamental values, it is important to assert a consistent set of company values worldwide."

The article continues: At the Cabot Corporation, concerns about employee safety are very high in the production of carbon black. In other countries, with differing health and safety standards, one might think a company operating there would adjust accordingly. "Cabot president Samuel Bodman asserts, 'We have the same standards of safety in every plant we operate everywhere in the world. The first priority ... is the safety of our plants.' He went on to note that of the five Cabot plants with the best safety records, three are in Argentina, Malaysia, and the south of France."

Arthur D. Little cites another example. John Hancock moved into Southeast Asia where business and governmental practices that are questionable by Western standards are widespread. Stephan Brown, Chairman: "We just felt that things like payoffs were wrong—and if we had to do business that way, we'd rather not do business. Our employees would not feel good about having different levels of ethics. There may be countries where you have to do that kind of thing. We haven't found that country yet, and if we do, we won't do business there."[24]

When dealing internationally, maintaining a reputation can take the application of beliefs well beyond the call of duty. For example, at Levi Strauss: "In 1992, to square its international sourcing practices with its own ethical code, Levi's began cracking down on child-labor violations by enforcing International Labor Organization standards that bar employment of children under the age of 14. Two Bangladeshi contractors admitted to Levi's that they hired children and agreed to fire them. They also argued ... that the boys and girls provided their families' sole economic support.... Levi's could have ignored its code, or it could have canned the kids and forgotten about them. Instead, it worked out a compromise with the contractors: If they continued to pay wages and agreed to hire the children back when they turned 14, Levi's would send them to school and foot the bill for uniforms, books, and tuition.... But between the two, Levi's and its contractor have spent just a few thousand dollars.... 'In today's world a TV exposé on working conditions can undo years of effort to build brand loyalty,' says Haas. 'Why squander your investment when, with commitment, reputational problems can be prevented?'"[25]

As K-T's business expanded with subsidiaries in many areas and countries, seeing that our basic beliefs were understood and applied took extra effort. First, we carefully assessed in-depth those we considered to manage an area or a country. This was especially critical not only because of geographical distance and managing director authority, but also because they were nationals of those countries and brought beliefs from that culture. We needed to make sure they could understand our beliefs and adopt them as far as work. In the one or two instances we were not thorough enough, that came back to haunt us. Second, all involved helped make sure our beliefs were a part of the legal, financial, and business development plans and activities of any subsidiary. Third, constant monitoring of beliefs was done by all employees who had reason to visit and work with a subsidiary. That included being a part of the interview process for prospective subsidiary employees. We made beliefs a part of every meeting and conference of our worldwide associates. Last, Ben Tregoe and all corporate personnel had open doors.

IGNORING BELIEFS IN TROUBLED TIMES

When an organization is in deep trouble there is pressure to do anything to fight back, including ignoring beliefs. The bigger the trouble, the greater the pressure and panic. Financial investors put increasing focus on the short term. Never mind the strategy; if cash is the issue, sell off the winners. Cut costs by postponing research, maintenance, capital outlay, or hiring. Reengineer, downsize, outsource, and the like. Bring in a new CEO. Hire a consultant. Don't ever publicly admit a mistake, and set defenses against all who are involved with or promoting the trouble.

A major problem for many companies engaged in fierce global competition is cost reduction caused by past over-staffing. "'The advantage to head-count cuts is that they happen fast, and the markets tend to react favorably,' notes Kim S. Cameron, a professor at the University of Michigan business school. 'The disadvantage is that it's like throwing a grenade into a crowded room.' And Cameron has seen the fallout: Of the 150 restructuring companies he has studied, three-quarters end up worse off after their downsizing. Of course, many smaller companies have gone astray just like big ones and often it's for the same reasons: They build in too much bureaucracy as they get larger and lose touch with their employees and principal markets."[26]

"Apple Computer Inc., for one, largely abandoned career development after sluggish sales growth forced restructuring in 1994. 'Just as the [human resources staff] would gear up, they'd be hit with a layoff,' says an executive who worked on the program. 'Now, it's a mess.'"[27]

Goldman Sachs is another case in point. "In the wake of huge trading losses and the failure of a costly, poorly executed overseas expansion strategy, Goldman was firing employees by the busload, and many top partners were unexpectedly taking early retirement. The firm's vaunted collegial culture, nurtured by Weinberg [John Weinberg, semiretired senior chairman] and his father Sidney before him, was fracturing. Work in some areas of the firm's lower Manhattan headquarters nearly halted as traumatized employees who had just been dismissed were escorted to the door, a scene repeated at other Goldman offices in the U.S., Hong Kong, London, and elsewhere.

"A heavyset, grandfatherly figure who could pass for an old-fashioned New York cab driver, Weinberg was the embodiment of the old, family-oriented Goldman culture. He felt furious and heartsick, say several current and former employees: furious at what he felt was Friedman's [Stephen Friedman, now resigned successor chairman] unconscionable betrayal, and heartsick that by aggressively pursuing trading for its own account, the quintessential white-shoe Wall Street firm had strayed from its original mission of putting client interest before its own. That shift of emphasis was behind many of the firm's troubles."[28]

While nonmanagerial and hourly employee concerns must be carefully thought out and well handled, management cannot be forgotten: "Constant restructuring has become a fact of business life in this era of change. Well and good, but companies that don't acknowledge the stress that survivors undergo and support those who are in danger of burning out may find that their glistening, reengineered enterprises end up being run by charred wrecks.... What can companies do to help thousands of other valuable, experienced managers before they burn out and leave? The Levinson Institute's Kraines insists that the first thing top management must do is walk managers below them through all the steps that led to the decision to restructure the company. What was happening in the marketplace that made it necessary? Why did they have to reorganize in this way and not in some other? Were there mistakes made at the top? This kind of information can lessen the guilt and enhance the performance of the managers who stayed behind."[29]

These "fixes" should not be considered in a vacuum. Any proposed action should be reviewed in light of its impact on beliefs that guide longer-term strategies, operations, and the capabilities to support them. That was the story at Manugistics. Management felt the greater the problem, and thus the more extreme the action, the more important it is to relate to your beliefs. After a successful merger, Manugistics faced a softening market with customer buying decisions delayed: "... [T]he management team at Manugistics was determined to take prudent actions, but actions that would be in keeping with the Elements of Excellence. Management team members felt that trust was never so important as it was in a time like this. Indeed, the team felt that if it didn't act in line with the company's values, employees would feel betrayed, and retention and productivity would be affected negatively."

Management moved quickly to alert employees. William Kaluza, CFO, explains: "Some people may not agree with the direction you take, but no one will disagree with the decision to share the information and the underlying justifications."

First, they got employee suggestions on how to reduce expenses and recognized and rewarded those they adopted. It was not enough, and ultimately a 13 percent reduction in workforce was required. Management decided that in this time of upheaval the Elements of Excellence would guide decisions about who was to be affected. It protected development and maintenance functions, which are usually deeply downsized.

Considerable support and help was given to those released: severance pay; use of company phone and e-mail; secretarial service; assistance in job seeking; a hotline to call back to the company; a referral network of job leads; a six-month follow-up program; expedited references, retirement disbursements, and unemployment claims. Managers received training to help both those affected and those not to deal with the situation: "'We were open with employees all along the way ... there wasn't the level of shock and surprise you usually see when a reduction in workforce occurs,' says Skelton [Tom Skelton, COO]."

The article describes the benefits of this beliefs-driven approach to a most difficult situation:

- The company could take prudent actions and maintain its beliefs. That went a long way toward restoring morale, returning to high productivity, and maintaining commitment.
- The loss of very employable people after the reduction was 12.6 percent compared to an industry average of 20 percent.
- New products were released on schedule and marketing and sales efforts were expanded.

In summary: "Because the business strategy and corporate culture of the company were integrated, Manugistics was able to act in a prudent business fashion without sacrificing its core values. The compliance with its core values enables an organization to strengthen the bond of trust with employees and clients and provides reassuring continuity in a time of bewildering change. A company's ongoing support of its core values helps employees and clients believe that things will get better, as long as they work together in a supportive fashion. Paying attention to consistency and values during difficult times may seem like a costly short-term commitment of time and resources, but the results can be more dramatic and produce a quicker return than any other investment a firm can make."[30] That is a pretty good way to get through a crisis, maintain your beliefs, and strengthen long-term loyalties and results.

THE ARROGANCE OF SUCCESS CLOUDS BELIEFS

Beliefs significantly influence sustained success. IBM and General Motors are classic examples. They had beliefs that helped lead them to the top of their industries. Then beliefs like serving the customer seemed to fade. So successfully entrenched and powerful, the companies ignored emerging new ways to fill their customers' needs. In their arrogance, they would essentially decide what the customer needed. And at IBM some of those new ways to serve customer needs were being developed right within the company. They just didn't receive very high priority. Fortunately for them, they were big and strong enough, bled enough, and changed enough to survive. But this pitfall can hit a company of any size, and most don't have IBM's or GM's resources and staying power. Results could be more disastrous. They could be fatal!

Eastman Kodak Company provides another example. In the past, Kodak's beliefs about quality, the customer, and technology led it to an enviable position. Then it went to sleep: "Kodak has spent billions on research and development, diversification, and repeated restructurings. Fisher's [George Fisher, new CEO, and ex-CEO of Motorola] immediate predecessor, Kay R. Whitmore, implemented no fewer than three reorganizations—yet Kodak earned less in 1993 than it had in 1982. Although blessed with a powerhouse brand name, it seemed trapped in the slow-growth photography industry, hobbled by huge debts, a dysfunctional management culture, and a dispirited workforce."

Fisher is shaking up the giant. He tackled the matrix management system which deflected responsibility for poor performance. He changed slow decision making and lack of risk taking by focusing on quality, customer needs, and shorter product development times: "The push for quick decision making is part of a broad campaign by Fisher to overhaul Kodak's lethargic culture. When Fisher arrived, he found an insular company that venerated authority and frowned on confrontation. 'It was so hierarchically oriented that everybody looked to the guy above him for what needed to be done,' he says.

"Fisher has turned himself into an ambassador of informality. Low-key, genial, he almost never raises his voice or shows anger. Fisher is far more accessible and visible than previous Kodak CEOs. He pops in on researchers for updates on projects and chats casually with staffers in the cafeteria. Employees are invited to send him E-mail messages, and they do—as many as 30 a day. He usually responds the next day with hand-written notes on the printouts."[31]

Intel provides a very specific example. As exemplified by CEO Andrew Grove, Intel had an open and proactive culture leading to sales of $20 billion and absolute dominance in the market for microprocessors. "Intel is so thoroughly focused on the Herculean task of doubling the number of transistors on its chips every 18 months that it has trouble seeing much else. Its vision is further obscured by a certain macho arrogance born of its market dominance. 'The culture, the centralized power, the tremendous profitability—it's a blinding light,' says venture capitalist Jack C. Carsten, former Intel senior vice-president. Concedes Grove in his crisp Hungarian accent: 'Sometimes you need a real jolt to realize a reality has kind of happened around you. We have to learn some skills that are second nature to others.' ... Intel's response to the Pentium problem was classic Andy Grove—by turns relentlessly aggressive, coldly analytical, and angrily defiant. He calmly explained that, by Intel's calculations, the problem occurs too rarely to concern any but the most demanding scientists. When critics came up with examples of more frequent errors, Grove shot back: 'If you know where a meteor will land, you can go there and get hit.' He finally acquiesced with a replacement policy, but not until IBM launched an embarrassing broadside: Big Blue announced it would stop selling Pentium PCs after releasing its own test results claiming the chip failed more often than Intel was saying."[32]

Recognize that when trouble occurs, the very power of the beliefs that produced great success must be turned toward correcting the trouble. There is a fine line between using those beliefs to overcome real trouble and letting them act as blinders that allow you to deny it. Keeping beliefs driving strategic and operational decision making when you are winning may be just as difficult as seeing their potential power when you are in trouble.

With a basic beliefs process in place and the pitfalls recognized and addressed, let's conclude with a few challenges that need careful thought and attention.

CHALLENGES AHEAD

Challenges are broad issues that develop from all the external and internal change that affects business and the world in general. They don't suggest a right or wrong answer. How any one of them might affect a particular organization or individual and how it should be addressed require serious thought. I present a number of challenges here, in the context of addressing them with a focus on basic beliefs and the basic beliefs process.

LOYALTY VERSUS ATTRITION

In the past, a company's beliefs and performance produced pride and loyalty. That was a rock-solid platform for satisfied, motivated, and productive employees. There was security born of individual performance and corporate success. That's what used to be; it's not so today. Now there is widespread insecurity about one's job, regardless of performance. And this leads to a broader insecurity: What are the company's real beliefs about people? This situation breeds fear, which can make beliefs about teamwork, honesty, and the long term a myth.

Opinion is divided on what to do with this challenge. Some say the past is dead. Give employees the best, up-to-date skills and knowledge, and then make them more responsible for keeping or finding a job anywhere—with the focus on "anywhere." Keith Hammonds, writing in *Business Week*, elaborates on this general idea: "Employability begins with the premise that any guarantee of job security is anachronistic. Instead, a new sort of 'contract' has emerged between employer and worker. Employees are responsible for their career development and for acquiring the skills they need to keep a job or land a new one. Companies are obliged to provide career resources and opportunities for training. If and when layoffs come, employees have an escape route. The idea rings appealingly of Emersonian self-reliance: Individuals who take an interest in their own advancement will thrive. Companies that invest in training, likewise, will realize productivity gains. In fact, 'leading-edge companies have been doing a lot of this work for a long time,' says Curtis E. Plott, president of the American Society for Training & Development."[1]

The same challenge occurs at the executive level: "Today's best young executives neither expect nor want a lifelong career at a single company. Employers do well to recognize that, and to emphasize the value to the individual of the work experience they offer. Says Andrea Miles, manager of employee selection and staffing at Corning Inc.: 'It has become more and more important to let people know that you are offering them a chance to develop skills that are marketable anywhere.'"[2]

On the other side, the Hammonds' article quoted above goes on to punch a hole in this concept: "But as a fix for economic anxiety, employability misses the point. By declaring upheaval unavoidable—and requiring employees to prepare for it—companies unburden themselves of any commitment to provide stable jobs. 'What employers are articulating is that they are no longer going to be responsible for their part of the bargain,' says Peter D. Cappelli, a professor at the University of Pennsylvania's Wharton School."

The article goes on to mention others who say we should strive to keep the old feelings of loyalty or get them back: "Companies such as Lincoln Electric and Nucor Corp. propose a different solution to economic turbulence. They provide consistent employment, no matter what, by working and managing better. 'Thinking ahead and having creative solutions for when there is a downturn is what management is all about,' Hastings [Lincoln Electric CEO Donald F. Hastings] said. Utterly naive?

Ask Pella Corp., a 3,500-employee window manufacturer in Pella, Iowa. Executives overhauled operations in 1994, cutting production times by two-thirds with no layoffs. 'No one worried about losing their job, so [employees] created change instead,' says consultant Anand Sharma, who advised the company. Certainly, better skills and continuing career development will make workers feel better about the future. 'If we tried to cut back on it, our hourly workers would kill us,' says just-retired Chairman James R. Houghton, of Corning Inc. By all means, keep the training, which ultimately is what makes business competitive. But employees would feel better, and be more productive, knowing that their employer won't show them the door at the first sign of trouble."[3]

I don't know whether loyalty or employability will win out over time. I think the worst case is to ignore this challenge. My bias would lean toward those organizations that think ahead and make decisions that nurture beliefs about loyalty and dedication. Somehow that seems the better way to reach sustainable, positive, long-term results.

Other consultants support my point of view: "His [Frederick Reichheld, Director, Bain & Co.] message is simply this: The best, most profitable employers are those that inspire loyalty among three constituencies: customers, investors, and employees. The lower the turnover of these three, the higher the company's profits. And—this is important—the lower the turnover of employees, the lower the turnover of customers and investors.... People become more productive (and thus more valued) when they stay with the same company for a long time because they learn how to do their job better, how to reduce costs and improve quality. This holds true in almost all fields."[4]

If you can combine this kind of loyalty with longevity, no one will beat you. Says Raymond W. Smith in *Fortune*: "It also takes a special kind of company to nurture a climate of open, frank, and relentlessly objective discussion so that all the variables are scrutinized honestly and without political repercussions. The loyalty required in this system differs subtly but crucially from the loyalty that prevails in most hierarchical organizations. This is loyalty not to one's own advancement or one's boss or one's department, but to the truth as it bears on the goals of the organization."[5]

On the other hand, in some businesses the "prepare for in-or-out employability" side of the challenge is viable: organizations with high levels of mobility—such as high-tech firms, professional organizations, commission-driven businesses, new and fast-growing industries. In those situations, where loyalty to profession is often higher than loyalty to firm, keeping skills updated is the best hope. This will ensure creativity, motivation, and productivity whether you work in one firm or another. If the application of merit beliefs is producing strategic success and if the application of ethic beliefs is producing an effective and satisfying work environment, you have a good chance to reduce mobility in any situation. Whichever way you go, make sure your beliefs support that direction.

RESTRUCTURING VERSUS EMPOWERMENT

Warren Bennis, Distinguished Professor of Business Administration at the University of Southern California, said in a recent editorial: "Empowerment and restructuring are on a collision course…. Unless the private sector finds a way both to make money and re-establish a sense of trust in the workplace, we'll continue to be in trouble." He adds that, "It's impossible for a company to re-engineer and empower at the same time, even though many firms are attempting it."[6] I agree with his collision analogy but not with his second conclusion.

Julie Connelly, writing in *Fortune,* says it another way: "An important proximate cause of heightened incivility is reengineering, by now the Great Satan of corporate life…. When incivility becomes the norm, the effect on companies is the moral equivalent of red ink. Mentoring, the way the corporate culture is passed down from worker to worker, declines. Why take the risk of helping someone who might snatch your job?"[7]

Mike Hammer, author of *The Reengineering Revolution,* says: "The real cause of reengineering failure is not the resistance [to change] itself, but management's failure to deal with it."[8]

For example, Chase Manhattan used to have beliefs devoted to job security and loyalty. Then the focus for these beliefs changed. The emphasis was placed on providing ongoing skills for employees to allow them to succeed at Chase *or* somewhere else. Then came the merger with Chemical Banking Corporation and a further wave of downsizing. Here is the comment of a survivor: "The merger has eliminated for me a certain motivation and all risk-taking, because this boy was a risk-taker. I went into areas that no one else wanted to go into. I did a lot of confrontation and tried my best to make it constructive and change things.... I'm not doing that any more. We've all become soldiers. We will obey whatever is said and will not challenge. Since the merger, it's just a 9-to-5 job for me."[9] How much short- or long-term contribution will that attitude provide?

Mitchell Marks of Delta Consulting Group points out that loyalty is one of the first casualties of downsizing: "The workers most stung by the seeming injustice of such cuts are often the most loyal—the sort of people who stay late and take special trouble with new recruits. Having carelessly lost that loyalty, companies have started to realize just how valuable, and how hard to restore, it really is. Able employees jump ship at the first opportunity."[10]

When you guide your actions by basic beliefs you must have the patience and perseverance to make them work. That is true both for those who manage and those who are a part of the action. Empowerment and teamwork can be alien, uncomfortable concepts for those who have spent their working life taking orders. Instead of grouping workers by function, they are now often grouped in teams with responsibility for a broader output. Incentive pay is tied to team performance rather than the more typical individual reward system. When a team member is not contributing his or her fair share, things can get out of whack in a hurry. "After 18 months of teamwork in El Paso [at a Levi Strauss plant], turnaround time from order to shipment has dropped from seven days to three. But the workers aren't all getting along.... A poor performer or absent worker affects everybody's paycheck.... Supervisor Gracie Cortez says that 'it gets tough out there.' She finds herself intervening to prevent 'big fights.' Says plant manager Edward Alvarez: 'Peer pressure can be vicious and brutal.' ... [P]lant workers got two weeks of training before the team system kicked in, part of it devoted to group dynamics. Alvarez allows it 'wasn't enough. We're trying to find a more effective way to do it.'"[11]

Beliefs can be used to organize, train, and motivate employees so they will seek ways to improve productivity, create new products and product improvements, and strengthen customer relationships, all to improve revenues. People can be empowered to help control downsizing. "Lyles [Royce Lyles] was managing director of JEA [Jacksonville Electric Authority] from 1979 to 1995.... By the mid-1980s, JEA was out of survival mode.... At JEA he [Lyles] began building—not just a crisis-control approach, but a new culture. Performance ... was measured on charts and graphs. Where action was quantified, room for improvement magically appeared, visible to men and women doing the job.... The JEA dictatorship of old was opened up. Trust was built among employees.... Yet there were no forced layoffs. JEA had downsized as it grew. Today the top-rated utility in the nation has one fewer employee than in 1979 when there were 100,000 fewer customers."[12]

When downsizing or restructuring is required in an organization that champions beliefs like empowerment, successful practitioners use those very beliefs to ease and reduce the obvious pain. Robert D. Haas, Chairman and CEO of Levi Strauss & Company, describes it this way: "Sometimes, the only solution is to close a plant, and if we don't have the guts to face that decision, then we risk hurting a lot of people—not just those in one plant.... 'How are we going to treat people who are displaced?' ... We give more advance notice than is required by law. We provide more severance than is typical in our industry.... We extend health care benefits. We also support job-training programs and other local initiatives to help our former employees find new jobs. And in the community itself, which has been depending on us as a major employer, we continue for a period of time to fund community organizations and social causes that we've been involved with.... The Aspirations [Levi's basic beliefs statement] make us slow down decisions.... There have been plants we have decided not to close, even though their costs were higher than other plants we did close.... The Aspirations also provide a way to talk about these difficult trade-offs inside the company.... That forces us to be explicit about all the factors involved. It causes us to slow up, reflect, and be direct with one another about what's happening."[13]

Decentralization, team or project groups, and individual empowerment are powerful approaches to gaining the highest levels of motivation, thinking, quality, productivity, and loyalty from any employee. On the other hand, there is the anxiety, mistrust, and concern for security regardless of performance caused by massive downsizing. The real issue in downsizing is how to handle it when it is necessary. "When it is necessary" should be after all other approaches to cost reduction have been accomplished, strategic options to increase revenue have been initiated, and consequences to long-term viability have been addressed. "How to handle it" successfully requires a full application of basic beliefs about people.

Companies that find downsizing necessary to survive in this fiercely competitive world have two choices. First, they can use their beliefs to be honest and open about what is going on and why, and make decisions that are least painful for those who are going and less anxious for those who are staying. Second, they can just "do it" with only the proposed cost gains in mind, forgetting the emptiness of those who are leaving and the mistrust of those who are staying. Often those that make the second choice are worse off after the downsizing than before.

For companies that make the first choice, an honest management, when appropriate, must take part of the blame for past uncontrolled hiring practices when everything was going up. Management must also take partial blame for not keeping employees' skills up to the requirements of changing times. There is no point in looking back unless it helps the future. Better structure and control of job creation at all levels and application of beliefs about people—training and development, recognition and reward for creativity, team building, tapping the potential of all employees—would have prevented some of the carnage of three million workers laid off, 77 percent white-collar, from 1978 to 1996. Put in context with eight million jobs created in the past four years, 60 percent managerial and professional, I can't help but wonder if a little better application of belief in "people are our most important asset" wouldn't have reduced the tremendously costly gap between those who were not prepared and were let go, and the new, qualified breed coming in. Would the total dollar cost for training and upgrading job skills for the three million employees lost cost more than finding, orienting, and placing three million of the eight million that came in? I raise the question knowing that all of the three million laid off would not fit within the eight million jobs created, under the best of circumstances.

Of course, this scenario could be all wrong. If the *only* reason for downsizing is to get rid of more senior and higher-paid employees and replace them with more junior and less expensive employees, then beliefs in people are dead.

A thoughtful application of basic beliefs should help address the challenge of doing necessary downsizing in a way that doesn't destroy or drive a wedge into the benefits of empowerment.

CEO PAY VERSUS EMPLOYEE PAY

This statement on the cover of the April 21, 1997 *Business Week* highlights this challenge: "Executive Pay—It's Out of Control. By relying heavily on stock options, many companies make exorbitant payouts for so-so performances, dilute real shareholder return, and glorify CEOs at the expense of other employees. The bottom line: Don't confuse a bull market with managerial genius."

This quote from the article in that issue presents the other side: "Despite the soaring pay, many experts argue that the system is working better than ever. They see the bull market and healthy corporate sector as proof positive that companies get what they pay for. They argue that as long as CEOs continue to turn in strong results for their shareholders, the absolute level of executive pay is irrelevant."

And too often this rationalization is made: "'When stock prices go down [CEOs argue], it's purely the vagaries of the market,' says Kevin Murphy, a professor of business administration at USC. 'But, when they go up, it's what they did to create value.'"[14]

Two major issues make up this challenge: first, directly relating the majority of the CEO's compensation to meeting and exceeding tough goals and creating real value versus "so-so performance"; second, insuring that all employees' contributions to achieving those goals are recognized and the results shared in equitable ways, which often does not appear to be the case.

Failure to address the pay challenge may eventually kill the spirit of basic beliefs. Warren Bennis, University of Southern California, leads into this challenge as he describes the growing disparity between the nation's rich and poor. "In the middle of the 1970s, the income gap between the very rich and the very poor was at its narrowest: 1 percent of the population controlled 18 percent of private wealth; now, 1 percent of the population controls 40 percent of the wealth. Corporations reflect the same widening gap between the haves and have-nots. There is a colossal disparity between the average pay of CEOs and the pay of the average worker; estimates of the ratio range up to 140-to-1. The disparity persists even in adverse times. While CEOs walk away from mergers and other corporate upheavals with multi-million dollar golden parachutes, the downsized thousands get a few months' severance pay and lose sleep over their health care coverage."[15]

Marjorie Kelly, Publisher of *Business Ethics,* makes this point: "And compared to 1985 workloads, employees now do the work of 1.3 people.... If we had the money to show for it, we might feel all right.... At the end of 1995, average weekly earnings were the lowest in 30 years, according to no less an authority than Barron's.... For 13 years in a row ... productivity climbed faster than real compensation.... Alan Sinai, Chief Economist at Lehman Brothers, added: 'Never in our history have American workers been asked to do so much for so little.'"[16] No wonder workers are mistrusting and upset. Faith in beliefs fades.

For some companies the sacrifices and rewards along the way need to be brought into better balance. John A. Byrne writes using data from *Business Week's* 1995 Executive Pay Scorecard of top-paid executives at 362 of the largest corporations: "Net income [at United Technologies] rose 28%, to a near-record $750 million on $22.8 billion in sales." Shareholders gained 55 percent in 1995. Chairman Daniell received $11.2 million. Sounds fine, but: "Listen to a United Technologies Corp. manager in the trenches who has seen his company downsize by some 30,000 employees in the past six years: 'I used to go to work enthusiastically,' he complains. 'Now, I just go in to do what I have to do. I feel overloaded to the point of burnout. Most of my colleagues are actively looking for other jobs or are just resigned to do the minimum.' Despite consistently good performance reviews, this $64,000-a-year manager with nearly two decades of service to the company has averaged a mere 4% pay raise in each of the past three years. 'At the same time, the CEO is paid millions, and his salary is going up much higher than anyone else's,' he adds. 'It makes me angry and resentful.'" If that attitude predominates down the line, there won't be much of a motivated workforce to contribute to anyone's compensation rewards.

Byrne continues: "In the past five years, average CEO pay has gone up 92% while corporate profits have risen 75%. So why all the hand-wringing over rising executive pay? The reason is simple: Few of these gains have trickled down to the hourly wage earners, supervisors or even the middle managers." To demonstrate, the article makes these points. Where appropriate, the 1996 *Business Week* Annual Pay Survey results have been added in parentheses following the 1995 figures.

- "Factory worker pay is up only 16% since 1990.
- The average salary and bonus for a chief executive rose by 18% in 1995 (39% in 1996), to $1,653,670 ($2.3 million in 1996)—slightly above the 15% gain in corporate profits. But throw in gains from long-term compensation such as stock options, and the CEO's average total pay climbed 30% in 1995 (54% in 1996), to $3,746,392 ($5,781,300 in 1996). The boss's pay not only outstripped last year's 2.8% inflation rate, but also the pay of both white-collar professionals, who averaged a 4.2% gain in 1995 (3.2% in 1996), and of factory employees, who received a 1% raise (3% in 1996).
- In 1980, the boss's average paycheck was a mere $624,996—42 times the pay of the ordinary factory worker. In 1995, the multiple had grown to 141 (209 in 1996).
- The CEOs of the 20 companies with the largest announced layoffs last year saw their salaries and bonuses jump by 25%, well above the average. Add the value of new stock-option packages granted to these same CEOs in 1995, and the increases are often staggering."

The article concludes: "A 1992 study of 89 organizations that made products ranging from kitchen appliances to truck axles found lower product quality in outfits with the widest gaps in pay. 'These organizations weren't able to sustain a workplace of people with shared goals,' explains David I. Levine, co-author of the study and a professor at the Haas School of Business at Berkeley." And "... executives had little choice but to respond to the pressure to perform. Today they are enjoying the rewards for a job well done. But the jury's still out on what the long-run consequences of their actions will be for America's corporations and their workers."[17] Careful thought on the relationship of beliefs to decisions about compensation will help bring in a jury verdict of not guilty.

It appears that some CEOs just don't see the impact of their compensation on worker motivation down the line, as those workers think about beliefs such as honesty, fairness, sharing, and participation. Byrne writes in another *Business Week* article: "New CEO pay figures make top brass look positively piggy. The CEO's [Robert Allen] basic pay didn't climb, but an option grant valued at $11 million enraged critics in a year when AT&T announced massive layoffs and shares rose only 28.9%. Aetna shares rose 46.9% last year, aided by the sale of its property and casualty unit. But Compton's [Chairman Ronald Compton] compensation far out-paced that, rising 485%." Boards of directors get in the act: "New proxy rules—set three years ago—forced boards to spell out specific goals that would unleash incentive pay. To preserve their flexibility, many simply increased payouts and often lowered targets." And an interesting consequence: "Given the magnitude of their pay hikes, CEOs look like easy game for pols on the stump. That goes double if they come off as insensitive to the travails of average wage earners during an era of downsizing and employee disenchantment. 'Politicians could start talking about raising tax rates for high-income individuals,' says David N. Swineford, a pay expert."[18] The reputation of business in general is tarnished when some top managers violate any concept of fairness in compensation.

But let's be reasonable. The CEO, as the ultimate decision maker, should be amply rewarded for performance that increases the value of the corporation for all stakeholders. Part of that value comes from getting labor costs and productivity in line to meet global competition. That helps assure the survival and future of the organization. The point has been made that the CEO and top management should use the intent of basic beliefs to ease the pain of downsizing. When that is done right the board and top management give careful consideration to the following CEO decision areas, concerns about disparities and fairness in compensation diminish:

- Makes strategic decisions to increase the revenue stream in balance with operating decisions to improve effectiveness.

- Adds economic value to the organization consistently over time.

- Shares that value with all stakeholders—employees, management, investors, and customers.

- Keeps needed short-term actions in line with beliefs and in support of long-term goals.

- Holds his or her base salary in more reasonable balance with the average worker and takes more compensation in options, bonuses, and the like pegged to long-term value creation.

- Personally invests and holds stock in the company in significant degree.

- Determines "golden parachutes" as part of a total severance policy.

Very broad reputational points are gained when these kinds of actions are taken and made known.

There are some encouraging signs that this challenge is being addressed. The previous article goes on: "In 1995, nearly 50% of all the companies in a survey by Towers Perrin had cobbled together some form of variable-pay plan for nonexecutives—nearly double the share that did so four years ago. An additional 26% said they were considering such plans. And a survey by human resources consultants Hewitt Associates found that companies budgeted an average 7.6% of payroll for results-sharing awards in 1995—up from 5.9% in 1993."

There are some cautions in considering variable-pay plans. As far as merit pay increases: "Indeed, some 20% of the businesses surveyed by Towers Perrin either reduced future merit-pay increases or froze base pay as they implemented pay-for-performance programs." Don't use different measures for executive and nonexecutive bonus schemes: "Fleet enraged employees, though, because Chairman Terrence Murray and other top managers received big year-end bonuses that weren't tied to the same measurements. 'We were being asked to make sacrifices, but they didn't do the same,' says Harrison F. Hazard, a former lending officer." Don't pick the wrong measures: "Sears, Roebuck & Co., for instance, stumbled in 1992 when it paid commissions to its auto-shop employees that were pegged to the size of repair bills. The result: overbilled customers, charges for work never done, and a scandal that tarnished Sears' reputation."[19]

There are many examples of better ways to apply beliefs and treat this challenge: "Chairman Max DePree and his forebears atop Herman Miller [office furniture manufacturer] have built a thriving enterprise in large part because of sturdy bridges between management and employees.... Max's father ... set the kinder, gentler tone with profit-sharing and employee-incentive programs long before they were fashionable." When Max stepped down as CEO, Richard Ruch, a 33-year veteran employee, became the first "outsider" to run the business. Max limited his salary to a figure 20 times the average pay of a line worker in the factory. "One of the keys to leadership is making sure you don't find yourself defending the wrong things, such as your own inflated salary," Max said. Ruch professes no qualms about his salary limitations.[20]

This *Business Week* article supports the point: "... [T]he idea is to make workers' motivation consistent with that of managers and investors. 'We share the pain and share the gain,' says Nucor CEO John D. Correnti. At Nucor, every employee's pay depends on the steel maker's profitability." Joseph P. Sullivan, Chairman of fertilizer giant Vigoro Corp., limits his own salary to 20 times that of $25,000 entry-level workers. "'Everybody should pay if a company is having a bad year—or a bad decade,' he says."[21]

The most positive way to address this challenge is to consistently create real value in the corporation over time. "MVA [market value added] in effect shows the difference between the capital investors have put into a company and the money they can take out." Following are the top five in MVA for 1996: "Coca-Cola—$87.82 billion; General Electric—$80.79 billion;

Merck—$63.44 billion; Philip Morris—$51.63 billion; Microsoft—$44.85 billion."[22] If this value is appropriately shared by management, employees, and stockholders, no one is going to worry as much about pay disparities.

When anyone is unhappy over the fairness of compensation, and that unhappiness is justified, it can easily become a sore point of such magnitude as to cause one to mistrust all beliefs. Controlling this growing pay spread could go a long way toward rekindling and improving employee motivation and eliminating that mistrust.

THE ORGANIZATION AND THE FAMILY

Changing family structure and values have increasing impact on how the corporation interprets its beliefs and makes decisions about its people: "Far more than in the past, says Jose Berrios, vice president for diversity at Gannett, astute managers have to concern themselves with diverse employees' lives outside the workplace. You've got to know if someone's performance is slipping because of worries about the quality of the day-care center, or be ready to step in and offer the company's resources if a worker is bedeviled by a troubled teenager at home. Not all of today's workers can isolate family problems from the job. Berrios sees immediate and long-term payoffs for organizations that maintain an enlightened attitude toward work and family issues: 'First, it costs a lot more to replace effective employees who are temporarily distracted by personal matters. And in the long run, the companies that handle these problems extremely well will become the employers of choice in an ever tighter labor market.'

"That sort of thinking is gaining hold elsewhere as senior managers struggle to adapt to work force shifts. Du Pont recently conducted a study of employees' commitment to business success and the company's efforts to help workers balance work and family responsibilities. The study found that employees who were aware that Du Pont work-life programs could help them with problems like finding child care or elder care were 45% more likely to agree strongly that they will 'go the extra mile' to assure Du Pont succeeds."[23]

That is all to the good, but this is the challenge: "... the Conference Board in New York City notes that only 2 percent of employees use them [work family programs]. As University of St. Thomas Prof. Patricia Hedberg writes ... 'many employees are paranoid about losing their jobs.'"

Marjorie Kelly, publisher of *Business Ethics* and author of the article that included the previous quote, says: "How is it we set up 'friendly' programs that people are afraid to use? What are we doing to create an environment of mistrust? When we work employees harder than ever, lay them off in droves, and push productivity up, while we push wages down: What message are we sending?"[24]

A recent *Business Week* cover story, "Balancing Work and Family," states the challenge clearly. *Business Week*, together with the Center on Work & Family at Boston University, has conducted a year-long study: "The results add up to a compelling agenda for corporate managers. Yet they also reflect a yawning divide between family-friendliness in theory and in practice. While 48% of the 8,000 employees in *Business Week*'s survey said they could 'have a good family life and still get ahead' in their company, 60% reported that management didn't, or only 'somewhat' did, take people into account when making decisions. More telling, more than two-fifths said that work had a negative impact on their home lives. 'I may have flexibility to accommodate family needs ... but I'm home working until midnight to get my job done,' wrote one employee. Indeed, says Bradley K. Googins, director of the Center on Work & Family, 'while many companies offer benefits and programs, the underlying cultural issues still aren't very well addressed.'

"Typically, executives view work–family initiatives as inexpensive, politically correct gestures, easy accommodations to workers who otherwise have been slammed by stagnant wages, benefit cuts, and layoffs. Managers fail to buy in, and workers fear torpedoing their careers by appearing less than completely committed to their jobs.

"Employees acknowledge their companies' wealth of family-oriented programs but say they often don't do the job. Half of the respondents, and even more of high-paid managers and professionals, said they felt 'a lot' of stress and pressure at work.... Production and clerical workers, meanwhile, gave generally lower ratings, reflecting an undercurrent of tension distinctly at odds with the friendly cultures most participating companies say they promote. 'Most benefits are offered to managers, technical and office staff,' wrote one worker. 'Shift employees have no options.'"

Business Week answers the challenge by showing how the intent of basic beliefs needs reinterpretation and work practices need changing: "The bank [First Tennessee National Corp.] got rid of a lot of work rules and let employees figure out which schedules work best—'because they know what needs to be done' both on and off the job, says Becky Tipton, a department supervisor. Then it carted in a kitchen-sink-load of programs to ease family distractions, marketed them relentlessly, and sent Tipton and 1,000 other managers through 3½ days of training. In short order, clear gains in productivity and customer service emerged.... Higher retention rates, First Tennessee says, contributed to a 55% profit gain over two years, to $106 million.

"Aetna Life & Casualty Co. halved the rate of resignations among new mothers by extending its unpaid parental leave to six months, saving it $1 million a year in hiring and training expenses.

"At Motorola, which placed second in *Business Week*'s survey, a work-life vision statement is reinforced by regular training for supervisors and seminars for the rank and file, and by 50 professionals responsible for programs worldwide. It is translated into a set of benefits offered to workers across the company that reflects the company's values and business goals:

'Special Delivery' gives expectant parents a 24-hour nurse hotline, and a pager for dad in the last trimester; long-term care
insurance provides security for employees' extended families."

A study of Xerox, Corning, and Tandem Computer by the
Ford Foundation suggests "that successful solutions involved
rethinking work processes, rather than finding ways to make
people's lives fit the work: 'The usual way of dealing with families, individual negotiations between manager and employee,
was incomplete,' Massachusetts Institute of Technology Professor Lotte Bailyn says. 'We had to look at how work was
structured, at the culture around work, the norms, from the
point of view of people's families.'"[25]

To address this challenge, reinterpret the intent of your beliefs to include family values and needs as they relate to work.
Modify your work practices accordingly. Then, use those same
beliefs to put employees at ease so they will use the programs
provided. This is not just nice to do—it's a competitive edge.

TOWARD A BASIC BELIEFS "P&L"

This challenge will need top management initiation and support and the best creative energy of those who pursue the idea.
Quality reports, budget variances, sales analyses, P&L statements, the balance sheet, and the like are used as key indicators of a corporation's vitality and health. They focus on numbers and are used at all levels in the corporation. But the health
and vitality of the corporation as a whole and in its various
business units can be measured in another way: How are we
performing on basic beliefs?

Measuring performance against beliefs can begin anywhere
in the corporation. Corporate management, functional groups,
and work units can experiment with and develop performance
reports on the application of beliefs as they apply to their level
and work output. Then, ideally, those reports will be reviewed
with the same critique, detail, and follow-through as the typical performance reports now in use. The end result is a report

that assesses how effectively beliefs are being applied and how to improve that performance. Such a report might look like this.

BASIC BELIEF	GOAL— WHERE WE WANT TO BE	ACTUAL— WHERE WE STAND	IMPROVEMENT PLANS	ACCOUNTABILITY
_____	_____	____	_____	_____
_____	_____	____	_____	_____

Measuring the effectiveness of some beliefs may be number-based or quantified. Other beliefs are measured by a desired level of satisfaction. For those a specific target for acceptable satisfaction should be stated. Then "actual" can be assessed, problems identified, and improvements made.

There are multiple sources to assess how well a belief is working: focus groups; customer satisfaction surveys; employee attitude surveys; multiple level relationships with customers, employees, suppliers, and the media; competitive practices; market research; "shopping visits"; exit interviews; complaint reports, and the like. Select the most appropriate source(s) for the beliefs measure being checked. Let's look at some measures by which three fairly common beliefs might be assessed.

Belief: Best customer service in our industry

Possible Measures:

- Product fits customer need
- Product delivers benefits promised
- Product has acceptable value-to-price ratio
- End-user satisfaction if different from customer
- Product meets standards
- Billing on time and correct
- Problems accurately corrected on time

- Warranties, returns, replacements honored
- Sales and service personnel professional, helpful, courteous
- Repeat business, our percent of total customer usage, new customer referrals
- Customer perception of beliefs and service compared to competition

Belief: Honesty in all we do

Possible Measures:

- Product or parts theft
- Tools or equipment theft
- Packaging/labeling accuracy
- Price/quality fit
- Personal computer use
- Hotline usage
- Grievances about fairness and honesty
- Expense report violations
- Misrepresentation in sales
- Overselling
- Kickbacks
- Level of gift acceptance
- Integrity of internal communication

Belief: Leading-edge technology and innovation

Possible Measures:

- Percent of revenue and profit from established versus new products over a time frame
- Basic research breakthroughs
- Level of current product improvements
- Employee suggestions received
- Employee suggestions acted on, dollar savings

- Percent of revenue allocated to basic/applied R&D versus industry norms
- Retention of technological personnel
- Computer-based systems in place, dollars spent, scope, newness
- Competitive position
- Awards received
- Patent/copyrights granted
- Number of PhDs employed
- Papers presented to industry associations
- Number/scope of project teams working on new ideas

I don't know how much time or energy should be devoted to developing this kind of review of corporate vitality and viability. But reasonable effort to upgrade the evaluation of beliefs to a level approaching that given to strategy and operations should keep or lead an organization to "visionary" status. That means continued short-term success with that success contributing to sustained growth and profitability.

THE NEED FOR BELIEFS IN LIFE BEYOND WORK

With an understanding of the importance of beliefs and how they impact the world of work, another challenge is to take that insight to the world outside. While this is somewhat beyond the intent of this book, those who work spend the majority of their time outside of work. There is a need for this same kind of thinking about beliefs in all aspects of our lives. Therefore, the connection is relevant enough to warrant this small digression.

America is a country rich in beliefs. We are generous with time and money. We take care of and plan for our families. We enjoy hard work, fair pay, and the satisfaction and quality of life they bring. We encourage innovation and adapt to change, all the while trying to maintain the best of our beliefs from our heritage. We are honest, trustworthy, and fair—there is a lot of the Boy Scout in all of us.

But in contrast to this, there appears to be a growing, darker side. What used to be "Work hard, keep your nose clean, sacrifice along the way, and you will have a great life" for some seems to be drifting toward "Take what you can get now, never mind how, and tomorrow will take care of itself." There are many examples of that drift. While there may be other contributing factors, a beliefs breakdown lurks behind each one.

- On the political scene, we have little faith in the beliefs of many elected officials and that lack of faith has been earned.

- In our public schools more and more money is spent to turn out students unequipped for the real world in many ways. While there is a strong effort toward character education in public schools, I am not suggesting certain beliefs be taught to students. Rather, the beliefs of the school system itself need to be addressed.

- On the family scene, often discussed and debated "family values" seem to be softening and sacred vows set aside in favor of abuse and divorce.

- Many young people are dropping out, destroying their minds and bodies, and taking their lives—too overwrought with pressure and depression to find the excitement and enjoy the process of growing up and becoming self-reliant.

- Working parents are so busy with what they are doing, they don't have time or have forgotten what life is really about.

- Senior citizens are in need of care and love, and many are not receiving them from family or friends.

- In the sport and entertainment fields it seems that for many who own, participate, or report, money and fame are everything. Many, given the chance, continue to violate the privilege and yet reap rewards and recognition. Role models are harder to find.

- Directors of major charitable organizations and various evangelists enjoy high living on moneys pilfered from donations intended to help those in need.

- Some who receive aid like food stamps, welfare, or aid to dependent children cheat those who have given to them. Some directors of those programs don't seem to care, or are in on the dole.

- Television and movies are filled with violence, sex, and often few redeeming features. The newest answer to the TV problem is a control to limit what can be seen: Beliefs replaced by electronics.

- In the reporting media, too often the "real news" is seeking and finding a hole in someone's character.

- There are those who feel it is okay to cheat on taxes and various claims. After all, it's our money and we're entitled.

What can be done to slow or reverse these disturbing and often belief-based trends? The vast majority of Americans, including those directly involved with the above scenarios, have sound and uplifting beliefs. We need to think through how to better apply the collective power of those beliefs to the above situations and to life in general—ethic beliefs about honesty, trust, fairness, equality, and legality and merit beliefs about goal setting, quality, productivity, and service. We need to put these kinds of beliefs and the basic beliefs process to work in society in as many creative ways as we can develop.

- Sit with our families and discuss the beliefs we have and how to apply and monitor them both at home and in all the areas family members are involved in.

- Raise questions to test and evaluate all our leaders or potential leaders on their beliefs and not just on their opinions on various issues.
- Show by action that we will not support organizations, leaders, participants, reporters, and the like whose behavior continues to violate notions of sound beliefs.
- Do whatever is safely and securely possible to make actions that violate sound beliefs known.
- Give more time and energy to those in dire straits who keep and practice sound beliefs. Let it be known that your support will cease for those in dire straits who practice unsound beliefs and don't try to change.
- Let those who alter or violate beliefs to take advantage in one area know that you will not trust their beliefs and behavior in any area.

The last point addresses the concept that a fundamental set of beliefs applies at work, at home, and in the community. Beliefs are not situational. This example illustrates the point.

George Billingsley, Sam Walton's tennis partner, relates: "For about ten years, Sam and I played tennis at high noon—usually on the court over at his house. I think he liked to play during lunch hour because he wouldn't dream of taking any of his associates away from their jobs to play. On the court, he was the most competitive player. He studied his opponents' games, and he knew our strengths and weaknesses as well as his own. If you hit a ball to Sam's forehand, that point was his. He would hit it cross court, and it was over.

"He loved the game. He never gave you a point, and he never quit. But he is a fair man. To him the rules of tennis, the rules of business, and the rules of life are all the same, and he follows them. As competitive as he is, he was a wonderful tennis opponent—always gracious in losing and in winning. If he lost, he would say, 'I just didn't have it today, but you played marvelously.'"[26]

I conclude the discussion of this challenge with an example from my own family experience. Two years ago, when my youngest son was to be married, he asked me to say a few words at his wedding. Unable to find a special reading, my wife, Charlotte, and I wrote down the beliefs we felt had guided us through forty-five years of wonderful marriage. They have been a benchmark for my decisions and behavior at work, at home, and in the community.

In sharing these beliefs I am not trying to set myself or my family apart or above or to suggest they are the "right" beliefs or that they should be your beliefs. I made lots of mistakes along the way, and still do! Each of those mistakes helped sharpen and strengthen my beliefs. Of course, the good things did too. It's the process that's important. If this stimulates your interest in that process, that's great.

Try to keep and live by good values and beliefs. Discuss, share, and seek agreement on those most critical to your lives. Your children will appreciate your having done this. Trust is vital. Do not break it.

Try to share and work together on those activities that should be shared. But retain your independence where that is called for. It is independence that gives satisfaction to sharing.

Try to be fair when you disagree. Disagreement means opposing positions are possible and that agreement should be reached with discussion. If it is a situation where it is important for the other's view to prevail, make your point and give in graciously. Don't debate those areas where you have strong and conflicting viewpoints. Regardless of the outcome, be done with it, smile, and move on.

Try to be honest with each other and tell the truth no matter how difficult the situation. Love can stand and overcome great quantities of poor judgment. It won't last long with lies.

Try never to go to sleep or off to work when you are angry with each other. It will ruin your day, and, of course, you never know about life's uncertainties.

Try to live below your standard of living. Salt enough away for the future. That's not easy when you are just starting out, but it is a habit that needs early cultivation. Too many live for today and think the future, or someone else, will take care of tomorrow. That's bunk!

Try to understand that getting through the rough spots that confront any marriage is not easy. It takes cool thought, much openness, and great effort every day. Each of you must give 120 percent to this relationship. Too many people just don't think it is worth it. But as we look back, nothing can come close to the love and strength of our family, to the growth we have achieved, to the wonderful things we have shared, to the places we have been, to our friends, and, best of all, to the love we still share and to the future. Those who don't make that effort will never experience anything at that level.

Try to enjoy your love for each other and have real fun as often as you can. It is having those times together that builds a relationship that can cope with adversity when it comes along.

Try to have a meaningful faith. Recognize that life and the world around it were created with more wisdom and care than exists in all mankind. Take the best care of your physical, mental, and moral health.

Try always to keep and strengthen the relationships with all of your family. No matter how busy, make time to communicate, share, and be together as much as possible. Those without a close family have missed one of life's greatest pleasures and comforts.

Try to share your good fortunes and talents with those who need or would appreciate your support and counsel. Next to your love for each other and your family, and the love of your children, nothing provides more pleasure than giving of yourselves.

Try always to grow. Life is full of wonder and excitement. Keep those habits and practices that have meaning, but seek new opportunities and challenges that will extend your horizons. An old friend once said to me that "a rut is a grave with the ends knocked out."

We began each of these points with the word "try." We are far from perfect. We are still trying, and it is in that trying that levels closer to perfection are achieved.

Personal beliefs go to work and shape and strengthen corporate beliefs. Corporate beliefs go home and enrich personal beliefs. If we all take a pledge to put the power of beliefs to work in every facet of life in which we have an interest, and beyond that wherever we might be of help, we can conquer this challenge, given patience and time.

SUMMARY

I cannot find a better way to stress strategic and operational decision making through beliefs than to quote from a *Fortune* article by Frank Rose. He suggests that visionary thinkers are seeking a new paradigm for successful long-term business management: "Seventeen years ago sociologist Daniel Bell wrote that for most of human history, reality was nature; then it became technology; and now, in the postindustrial age of knowledge work and information science, it's the 'web of consciousness.' That is what's genuinely new about the new paradigm: this focus on human consciousness—not on capital or machinery, but on people. It has challenging implications. 'If consciousness is important then money and profit are no longer that important,' argues Michael Ray of Stanford. 'They're a way to keep score, but if you don't have any vision, you're not going to be successful in the long run. If you go for money and that's all, when you get it, there's nothing there.'

"So what's the alternative? Business as a spiritual pursuit? Don't laugh. Jack Welch recently remarked that he wants people at GE to feel rewarded 'in both the pocketbook and the soul.' This is the lesson of the new paradigm: If people are your greatest resource and creativity the key to success, then business results cannot be divorced from personal fulfillment. Which is why many executives may discover, as they arise from the hot tubs at Esalen, that when you eliminate the charlatans and strip away the bull, business and human potential are the same thing."[27]

I can only hope that with all the ideas and approaches suggested in this book, and those you will add, you are persuaded to take a fresh and probing look at your organization's basic beliefs process. Remember the key questions:

- Have all the beliefs been found?
- Which are really basic—essential to sustained success?
- Are they stated so all can understand and apply them?
- Are they communicated for commitment and application?
- Are they built in to be applied in every operation?
- What financial and nonfinancial recognition and rewards are in place for outstanding application?
- What disciplines or penalties are in place for lack of application?
- Does the monitoring program keep improving all aspects of the basic beliefs process?
- Is the intent of beliefs updated and kept in sync with changing times?
- Is the effectiveness of beliefs and the basic beliefs process reviewed as consistently and consciously as other results?
- Are all major strategic and operational decisions, plans, activities, and relationships guided by and in support of the basic beliefs?

In his masterpiece, *The Prophet,* the philosopher Kahlil Gibran said of teaching: "If he is indeed wise, he does not bid you enter the house of his wisdom but rather leads you to the threshold of your own mind."[28]

That has been my goal!

BASIC BELIEFS SURVEY

BACKGROUND AND PURPOSE:

Basic beliefs can significantly help an organization cope with major changes and provide for continued success and growth. Clearly articulating and embracing basic beliefs can help an organization to successfully cope with change. Your company has (*company name for beliefs*) or basic beliefs which guide its activities. A copy of these beliefs was attached to the cover memo of this survey.

The purpose of this survey is to help your company understand and improve how its beliefs are stated, communicated, applied, and reinforced. Your personal and individual thoughts and candid comments in responding to this anonymous survey will strongly guide those efforts.

Thank you very much for your thoughtful involvement.

INSTRUCTIONS FOR COMPLETING THE SURVEY:

For *questions with a scale,* circle the number of the response that best describes your answer.

For *questions that ask for a written response,* please be brief but specific.

While we want and need your best and candid thoughts, if you have no knowledge, experience, or feelings about a particular question, leave it unanswered.

When you have completed your survey, place it in the enclosed addressed and stamped envelope and mail it.

The survey should take approximately 30 minutes to complete.

BASIC BELIEFS SURVEY
(COMPANY NAME)

1. To what extent does management actively communicate the basic beliefs in the attached statement?

Not at All	Limited Extent	Moderate Extent	Considerable Extent	Great Extent
1	2	3	4	5

2. To what extent do you feel basic beliefs are used to guide day-to-day decisions and activities in your company?

Not at All	Limited Extent	Moderate Extent	Considerable Extent	Great Extent
1	2	3	4	5

3. To what extent are actions and behavior at the following levels influenced by the basic beliefs:

	Not at All	Limited Extent	Moderate Extent	Considerable Extent	Great Extent
	1	2	3	4	5
A. Senior Management ------	1	2	3	4	5
B. Mid-level Management ------	1	2	3	4	5
C. First Line Supervision --------	1	2	3	4	5
D. Nonmanagerial Work Force---------	1	2	3	4	5
E. Your Supervisor ---	1	2	3	4	5
F. Your Work Group --------------	1	2	3	4	5

4. Regardless of level, to what extent do successful people in the company more frequently follow and apply the basic beliefs than less successful people?

Not at All	Limited Extent	Moderate Extent	Considerable Extent	Great Extent
1	2	3	4	5

5. Please describe an important decision about which you feel the outcome was negative because the basic beliefs were not considered.

6. Please describe an important decision about which you feel the outcome was positive because it was strongly influenced by the basic beliefs.

7. Based on your own knowledge or experience, to what extent do basic beliefs *really* guide or influence:

	Not at All 1	Limited Extent 2	Moderate Extent 3	Considerable Extent 4	Great Extent 5
A. Relationships with customers ----------	1	2	3	4	5
B. Dealings with suppliers ------------	1	2	3	4	5
C. Advertising/selling products or services ------------	1	2	3	4	5
D. Relationships with the local community ---------	1	2	3	4	5
E. Relationships with stockholders -------	1	2	3	4	5
F. Relationships among employees ----------	1	2	3	4	5
G. Relationships with the union (optional)	1	2	3	4	5

8. To what extent are behavior and actions that support basic beliefs recognized and rewarded?

Not at All 1	Limited Extent 2	Moderate Extent 3	Considerable Extent 4	Great Extent 5

9. How are behavior or actions that support basic beliefs recognized and rewarded? Circle those appropriate.

   A. They are not

   B. Special, one-time cash bonus

   C. Considered in year-end bonus

   D. Considered in wage/salary increases

   E. Considered in job promotion

   F. Individual recognition by supervisor

   G. Special, noncash awards

   H. Recognition in company publications

   I. Other _____

   _____

10. To what extent are behavior and actions that conflict with basic beliefs discouraged or disciplined?

Not at All	Limited Extent	Moderate Extent	Considerable Extent	Great Extent
1	2	3	4	5

11. To what extent do you find yourself in work situations where you are expected to do something counter to the company's stated basic beliefs?

Not at All	Limited Extent	Moderate Extent	Considerable Extent	Great Extent
1	2	3	4	5

12. In important situations in your work and the work around you, when there is conflict between what is actually happening and the intent of the basic beliefs, what do you do about it?

   A. Go along with the situation as it is.

   B. Correct the situation OR bring it to the attention of someone who can do something about it.

13. To what extent do you feel conflict exists between the company's written basic beliefs and any other unwritten and informal beliefs that may be practiced?

Not at All	Limited Extent	Moderate Extent	Considerable Extent	Great Extent
1	2	3	4	5

14. How would you suggest your company's statement of basic beliefs be improved by changing the current wording?

15. How would you suggest your company's communication of basic beliefs be improved?

16. How would you suggest your company improve how it reinforces and rewards the application of basic beliefs?

17. Any other comments?

Strategy is a company's representation for becoming what it wants to be in the future regarding: scope and emphasis of products or services, customers, and geography; key capabilities required; and growth and return expectations.

(Note: Answer questions 18, 19, and 20 only if you have knowledge or experience in formulating company strategy.)

18. To what extent *are* basic beliefs considered in the development of your company's strategy?

Not at All	Limited Extent	Moderate Extent	Considerable Extent	Great Extent
1	2	3	4	5

19. To what extent *should* basic beliefs be considered in developing your company's strategy?

Not at All	Limited Extent	Moderate Extent	Considerable Extent	Great Extent
1	2	3	4	5

20. Briefly describe how basic beliefs *are* used in developing your company's strategy.

While your survey responses are anonymous, the following general information will be most helpful in analyzing and summarizing results.

21. Level

    1   Senior Management

    2   Mid-level Management

    3   First Level Supervision

    4   Nonmanagerial

22. Function

    1   Production/Maintenance

    2   Marketing/Sales/Customer Service

    3   Research/Design

    4   Support Staff (e.g., Finance, Human Resources, etc.)

    5   Other—Please describe:

    _____

23. Location

    1   United States

    2   Canada

    3   Latin America

    4   Europe

    5   Asia

24. Years with company

    1   Less than Three

    2   Three through Nine

    3   Ten or More

When you have completed the survey, place it in the enclosed addressed and stamped envelope, and mail it.

Thank you for your time and participation.

NOTES

CHAPTER 1

[1] Laurie Morse, "ADM agrees to $100 million fine for price-fixing," *The Knoxville News-Sentinel*, 15 Oct. 1996, p. C1.

[2] Thane Peterson, "Archer Daniels Indictments," *Business Week*, 16 Dec. 1996, p. 44.

[3] "The Corporation: The Fall of a Timber Baron," *Business Week*, 2 Oct. 1995, pp. 85-86.

[4] Richard Behar and Michael Kramer, "Something Smells Fowl," *Time*, 17 Oct. 1994, pp. 42-44.

[5] Terence P. Pare, "The Big Sleaze in Muni Bonds," *Fortune*, 7 Aug. 1995, pp. 113-20.

[6] Ron Stodghill II, "A Mea Culpa—and a Comeback?" *Business Week*, 3 July 1995, p. 33.

[7] Suzanne Barlyn and Kate Ballen, "Money and Markets/Cover Story: Untangling the Derivatives Mess," *Fortune*, 20 Mar. 1995, pp. 50-61.

[8] Kelley Holland, Linda Himelstein, with Zachary Schiller, "Cover Story: The Bankers Trust Tapes," *Business Week*, 16 Oct. 1995, p. 108.

[9] Willy Stern, "A Greater Threat Than Terrorism," *Business Week*, 9 Sept. 1996, pp. 86-90.

[10] Andrew Purvis, "The Goodwill Pill Mess," *Time*, 29 Apr. 1996, p. 64.

[11] "Texaco Settles for $176.1 M," *Florida Times-Union*, 16 Nov. 1996, pp. A1 and 6.

[12] Stewart Toy, "Under Suspicion: Le Tout Business Elite," *Business Week*, 22 Jan. 1996, p. 58.

[13] Karen Lowry Miller, "Something's Rotten in—Germany?" *Business Week*, 7 Aug. 1995, p. 44.

[14] John Rossant, "Twilight of the Gods," *Business Week*, 19 Aug. 1996, p. 52.

[15] Lindsay Chappell, "Web of Shame at Honda," *Automotive*, 31 Mar. 1994, p. 1.

[16] "Feds Shut Daiwa's Operations," *Florida-Times Union*, 3 Nov. 1995, pp. C8 and C11.

[17] Brian Bremner, "The Daiwa Coverup Will Backfire on the Banks," *Business Week*, 23 Oct. 1995, pp. 46-47.

[18] "Mr. Copper," *Minneapolis Star Tribune*, 15 June 1996, pp. D1-D2.

[19] Paula Dwyer, "Descent into the Abyss," *Business Week*, 1 July 1996, p. 28.

[20] "Sumitomo Trader," *Jacksonville Times-Union*, 20 Sept. 1996, p. C10.

[21] Mark Maremont, "Cover Story: Blind Ambition," *Business Week*, 23 Oct. 1995, pp. 81 and 91.

[22] Terence P. Pare, "Cover Story: Jack Welch's Nightmare on Wall Street," *Fortune*, 5 Sept. 1994, pp. 40-41.

[23] John A. Byrne, *Informed Consent* (McGraw-Hill, 1996), p. 6.

24 Ibid, p. 220.

25 Ibid, p. 225.

26 John Carey, "Breast-Implant Cases: Let the Science Testify," *Business Week*, 16 Dec. 1996, p. 40.

27 J. Madeleine Nash, "Ruling Out 'Junk Science,'" *Time*, 30 Dec. 1996–6 Jan. 1997, p. 102.

28 Benjamin B. Tregoe and John W. Zimmerman, *Top Management Strategy* (Simon and Schuster, 1980).

CHAPTER 2

1 Thomas A. Stewart, "It's a Flat World after All" (a review of the book *Beyond Reengineering* by Michael Hammer), *Fortune*, 19 Aug. 1996, pp. 197-98.

2 James C. Collins and Jerry I. Porras, *Built to Last* (Harper Business, 1994), p. 81.

3 Sam Walton with John Huey, *Made in America* (Doubleday, 1992), p. xiii.

4 Ibid, pp. 98, 134-41.

5 Barbara Fitzgerald-Turner, "A CEO places his faith in employees; CEO William M. Gibson of Manugistics Inc.," *Personnel Journal*, Oct. 1992, p. 44+.

6 Russell Mitchell with Michael Oneal, "Managing by Values," *Business Week*, 1 Aug. 1994, pp. 46-47.

7 Patricia Sellers, "Sears: In with the New," *Fortune*, 16 Oct. 1995, p. 98.

8 Brian O'Reilly, "J & J Is on a Roll," *Fortune*, 26 Dec. 1994, p. 178.

9 Ibid, p. 190.

10 Louis Kraar, "The New Power in Asia," *Fortune*, 31 Oct. 1994, pp. 88-96.

11 Russell Shaw, "Grounds for Success," *Sky*, Apr. 1995, p. 74.

12 Michael Ryan, "They Call Their Boss a Hero," *Parade Magazine*, 8 Sept. 1996, pp. 4-5.

13 Thomas Teal, "Not a Fool, Not a Saint," *Fortune*, 11 Nov. 1996, p. 204.

14 Gary Moore, "Miracle Man," *Jacksonville*, May 1996, pp. 24, 27, and 71.

15 Robert B. Reich, Steven D. Lydenberg, and Milton Moskowitz, "Should Investors Look Beyond the Bottom Line; considering workplace practices as indicators of corporations' future performance," *Business and Society Review*, 22 Sept. 1994, p. 6+.

16 Robert L. Gildea, "Consumer Survey confirms corporate social action affects buying decisions," *Public Relations Quarterly*, 22 Dec. 1994, p. 20+.

17 John E. Sheridan, "Organizational Culture and Employee Retention," *Academy of Management Journal*, 1992, pp. 1036-53.

18 Rahul Jacob, "Corporate Reputation," *Fortune*, 6 Mar. 1995, pp. 57-60.

19 "Chief Executive of the Year," *Chief Executive*, July/Aug. 1996, p. 50.

20 Rosabeth Kanter, "Values and Economics," *Harvard Business Review*, Sept.-Oct. 1990, p. 4.

21 James Krone Jr., "Do You Really Need a Mission Statement?" *Across the Board*, July/Aug. 1995, p. 17.

22 Robert Howard, "Values Make the Company: An Interview with Robert Haas," *Harvard Business Review*, Sept.-Oct. 1990, p. 134.

23 David Kirkpatrick, "This Tough Guy Wants to Give You a Hug," *Fortune*, 14 Oct. 1996, pp. 174 and 176.

24 Rosabeth Kanter, "Values and Ethics," *Harvard Business Review*, Sept./Oct. 1990, p. 4.

CHAPTER 3

[1] Russell Shaw, "Grounds for Success," *Sky,* Apr. 1995, p. 72.

[2] Barbara Fitzgerald-Turner, "A CEO places his faith in employees; CEO William M. Gibson of Manugistics Inc.," *Personnel Journal,* Oct. 1992, p. 44+.

[3] David Vogel, "Is U.S. business obsessed with ethics?" *Across the Board,* Nov. 1993, p. 30+.

[4] Barbara Fitzgerald-Turner, "Manugistics tests its values," *Personnel Journal,* Oct. 1992, p. 40.

[5] Charles M. Farkas and Philippe De Backer, "There Are Only Five Ways to Lead" (an excerpt from their book *Maximum Leadership*), *Fortune,* 15 Jan. 1996, pp. 109-11.

[6] Thomas J. Watson Jr., *Father, Son & Co.: My Life at IBM and Beyond* (Bantam Books, 1990), p. 302.

[7] Alan Farnham, "State Your Values, Hold the Hot Air," *Fortune,* 19 Apr. 1993, p. 118.

[8] Thomas A. Stewart, "Company Values That Add Value," *Fortune,* 8 July 1996, p. 148.

[9] Benjamin B. Tregoe, John W. Zimmerman, Ronald A. Smith, and Peter M. Tobia, *Vision in Action* (Simon and Schuster, 1989), p. 114.

[10] James C. Collins and Jerry I. Porras, *Built to Last* (Harper Business, 1994), pp. 68-69, 95.

[11] James Krohe Jr., "Do You Really Need a Mission Statement?" *Across the Board,* July/Aug. 1995, p. 21.

[12] Ibid, p. 21.

[13] Ibid, p. 18.

[14] Alan Farnham, "State Your Values, Hold the Hot Air," *Fortune,* 19 Apr. 1993, p. 118.

[15] Amy Barrett, "How Are You Voting? What Are Your Stocks?" *Business Week,* 28 Aug. 1995, pp. 66-67.

CHAPTER 4

[1] Rahul Jacob, "Corporate Reputation," *Fortune,* 6 Mar. 1995, p. 60.

[2] Ibid, p. 64.

[3] Robert Howard, "Values Make the Company: An Interview with Robert Haas," *Harvard Business Review,* Sept./Oct. 1990, p. 139.

[4] Stratford Sherman, "How Tomorrow's Best Leaders Are Learning Their Stuff," *Fortune,* 27 Nov. 1995, p. 100.

[5] Carolyn Wiley, "The ABC's of Business Ethics: Definitions, Philosophies and Implementation," *Industrial Management,* Jan. 1995, p. 22+.

[6] Robert Howard, "Values Make the Company: An Interview with Robert Haas," *Harvard Business Review,* Sept./Oct. 1990, p. 139.

[7] Stratford Sherman, "How Tomorrow's Best Leaders Are Learning Their Stuff," *Fortune,* 27 Nov. 1995, p. 93.

[8] Russell Shaw, "Grounds for Success," *Sky,* April 1995, p. 74.

[9] Kenneth Labich, "The New Crisis in Business Ethics," *Fortune,* 20 Apr. 1992, p. 176.

CHAPTER 5

[1] Thomas A. Stewart, "Why Value Statements Don't Work," *Fortune*, 10 June 1996, p. 137.

[2] Dee DePass, "Far More Than a Slap on the Wrist: Prudential to pay $35 million fine," *Minneapolis Star Tribune*, 10 July 1996, p. A9.

[3] Stratford Sherman, "How Tomorrow's Leaders Are Learning Their Stuff," *Fortune*, 27 Nov. 1995, p. 92.

[4] Lee Ginsburg and Neil Miller, "Value-Driven Management," *Business Horizons*, May-June 1992, p. 24.

[5] Ibid, p. 25.

[6] Alan Farnham, "State Your Values, Hold the Hot Air," *Fortune*, 19 Apr. 1993, p. 124.

[7] Richard A. Melcher, "How Goliaths Can Act Like Davids," *Business Week/Enterprise*, 1993, p. 199.

[8] Robert Howard, "Values Make the Company: An Interview with Robert Haas," *Harvard Business Review*, Sept.-Oct. 1990, pp. 138-39.

CHAPTER 6

[1] Lee Ginsburg and Neil Miller, "Value-Driven Management," *Business Horizons*, May-June 1992, p. 26.

[2] Robert Howard, "Values Make the Company: An Interview with Robert Haas," *Harvard Business Review*, Sept./Oct. 1990, p. 141.

[3] Kelley Holland, "A Chastened Chase," *Business Week*, 26 Sept. 1994, p. 107.

[4] Barbara Fitzgerald-Turner, "Manugistics tests its values," *Personnel Journal*, Oct. 1992, p. 40.

[5] Brian Dumaine, "Creating a New Company Culture," *Fortune*, 15 Jan. 1990, p. 130.

[6] Kenneth Labich, "The New Crisis in Business Ethics," *Fortune*, 20 Apr. 1992, p. 176.

[7] Carolyn Wiley, "The ABC's of Business Ethics: Definitions, Philosophies and Implementation," *Industrial Management*, January, 1995, p. 22+.

[8] Kenneth Labich, "The New Crisis in Business Ethics," *Fortune*, 20 Apr. 1992, p. 176.

[9] Rosabeth Kanter, "Values and Ethics," *Harvard Business Review*, Sept.-Oct. 1990, p. 4.

CHAPTER 7

[1] "The Big Picture: Boardroom Balance of Power," *Business Week*, 17 June 1996, p. 6.

[2] Richard A. Melcher and Greg Burns, "Archer Daniels Cleanup: Don't Stop Now," *Business Week*, 29 Jan. 1996, p. 37.

[3] Anne B. Fisher, "Making Change Stick," *Fortune*, 17 Apr. 1995, p. 124.

[4] Lee Ginsburg and Neil Miller, "Value-Driven Management," *Business Horizons*, May-June 1992, p. 24.

[5] Stratford Sherman, "How Tomorrow's Best Leaders Are Learning Their Stuff," *Fortune*, 27 Nov. 1995, p. 102.

[6] Amy Stevens, "Lawyers and Clients: Wall Street Turns to a New Breed of In-House Lawyer," *Wall Street Journal*, 14 Jan. 1994, p. B3.

[7] "Good Grief," *The Economist,* 8 Apr. 1995, p. 57.

[8] Richard Behar, "Stalked by Allstate," *Fortune,* 2 Oct. 1995, p. 128.

[9] Mark Maremont, "Abuse of Power," *Business Week,* 13 May 1996, pp. 88-89.

[10] Alison Rea and Leah Nathans Spiro, "Can Art Ryan Move 'The Rock'?" *Business Week,* 5 Aug. 1996, p. 71.

[11] Carolyn Wiley, "The ABC's of Business Ethics: Definitions, Philosophies and Implementation," *Industrial Management,* Jan. 1995, p. 22+.

[12] Kenneth Labich, "The New Crisis in Business Ethics," *Fortune,* 20 Apr. 1992, p. 176.

[13] Richard L. Osborne, "Strategic Values: The Corporate Performance Engine," *Business Horizons,* Sept.-Oct. 1996, p. 42.

[14] Richard Osborne, "Company with a Soul," *Industry Week,* 1 May 1995, p. 22.

[15] Kenneth Labich, "Why Companies Fail," *Fortune,* 14 Nov. 1994, p. 52.

CHAPTER 12

[1] Nick Gilbert, "1-800-22 Ethic," *Financial World,* 16 Aug. 1994, p. 25.

[2] "Exxon's Problems Not What You Think," *Fortune,* 23 Apr. 1990, p. 204.

[3] Diana B. Henriques, "Preaching but Not Practicing?" *The New York Times,* 22 Dec. 1995, p. D1.

[4] Linda Grant, "Rambos in Pinstripes: Why So Many CEOs Are Lousy Leaders," *Fortune,* 24 Apr. 1996, p. 147.

[5] Kenneth Labich, "Why Companies Fail," *Fortune,* 14 Nov. 1994, p. 68.

[6] "Editor's Notes in Your Interest: *Money* speaks out on a question of professional ethics," *Money,* Apr. 1995, p. 11.

[7] Ibid, p. 12.

[8] John F. Magee and P. Ranganath Nayak, "Leaders' Perspectives on Business Ethics: An Interim Report." *Prism,* First Quarter 1994, p. 65+.

[9] Shawn Tully, "Northwest and KLM: The Alliance from Hell," *Fortune,* 24 June 1996, pp. 64-72.

[10] Kenneth Labich, "When Workers Really Count," *Fortune,* 14 Oct. 1996, p. 214.

[11] N. R. Kleinfeld, "The Company As Family, No More," *The New York Times,* 4 Mar. 1996, pp. A1, A12, and A14.

[12] Geoffrey Smith, Phillip L. Zweig, and Alison Rea, "Time to Put Away the Checkbook," *Business Week,* 10 June 1996, pp. 97-98.

[13] Thomas J. Martin, "Jack Welch Lets Fly on Budgets, Bonuses, and Buddy Boards," *Fortune,* 29 May 1995, p. 147.

[14] Russell Shaw, "Grounds for Success," *Sky,* Apr. 1995, p. 69.

[15] Barbara Fitzgerald-Turner, "Manugistics tests its values," *Personnel Journal,* Oct. 1992, p. 40.

[16] Carolyn Wiley, "The ABC's of Business Ethics: Definitions, Philosophies and Implementation," *Industrial Management,* Jan. 1995, p. 22+.

[17] "Diversity," *Business Week,* 9 Dec. 1996, special section prior to p. 132.

[18] Ron Stodghill II, "Get Serious about Diversity Training," *Business Week,* 25 Nov. 1996, p. 39.

[19] Brian S. Moskal, "A Shadow between Values and Reality," *Industry Week*, 16 May 1994, pp. 23-24.

[20] Richard L. Osborne, "Strategic Values: The Corporate Performance Engine," *Business Horizons*, Sept.-Oct. 1996, p. 45.

[21] Barry Z. Posner and Warren H. Schmidt, "Values Congruence and Differences between the Interplay of Personal and Organizational Value Systems," *Journal of Business Ethics*, 1993, p. 346.

[22] Timothy K. Smith, "What's So Effective about Stephen Covey?" *Fortune*, 12 Dec. 1994, pp. 118-22.

[23] Richard Osborne, "Company with a Soul," *Industrial World*, 1 May 1995, p. 23.

[24] John F. Magee and P. Ranganath Nayak, "Leaders' Perspectives on Business Ethics: An Interim Report," *Prism*, First Quarter 1994, p. 65+.

[25] Russell Mitchell with Michael Oneal, "Managing by Values," *Business Week*, 1 Aug. 1994, pp. 51-52.

[26] Richard A. Melcher, "How Goliaths Can Act Like Davids," *Business Week/Enterprise*, 1993, p. 193.

[27] Keith H. Hammonds, "The Issue Is Employment, Not Employability," *Business Week*, 10 June 1996, p. 64.

[28] John S. Abbott, "Where Does Goldman Sachs Go from Here?" *Business Week*, 20 Mar. 1995, p. 104.

[29] Lee Smith, "Burned-Out Bosses," *Fortune*, 25 July 1994, p. 52.

[30] Barbara Fitzgerald-Turner, "Manugistics tests its values," *Personnel Journal*, Oct. 1992, p. 40.

[31] Mark Maremont, "Kodak's New Focus," *Business Week*, 30 Jan. 1995, pp. 63-65.

[32] Robert D. Hof, "The Education of Andrew Grove," *Business Week*, 16 Jan. 1995, p. 61.

CHAPTER 13

[1] Keith H. Hammonds, "The Issue Is Employment, Not Employability," *Business Week*, 10 June 1996, p. 64.

[2] Kenneth Labich, "Kissing Off Corporate America," *Fortune*, 20 Feb. 1995, p. 46.

[3] Keith H. Hammonds, "The Issue Is Employment, Not Employability," *Business Week*, 10 June 1996, p. 64.

[4] Marshall Loeb, "Wouldn't It Be Better to Work for the Good Guys?" *Fortune*, 14 Oct. 1996, p. 223.

[5] Raymond W. Smith, "Business As War Game: A Report from the Battlefront," *Fortune*, 30 Sept. 1996, p. 193.

[6] Warren Bennis, "Point of View: Workers' high anxiety about jobs may lead to era of social unrest," *Florida Times-Union*, 26 Feb. 1996, p. A17.

[7] Julie Connelly, "On Company Time: Have we become mad dogs in the office?" *Fortune*, 28 Nov. 1994, pp. 198-99.

[8] Anne B. Fisher, "Making Change Stick," *Fortune*, 17 Apr. 1995, p. 122.

[9] N. R. Kleinfield, "The Company As Family, No More," *New York Times*, 4 Mar. 1996, p. A12.

[10] "Friday Perspective, the Economist: Loyalty finds a place in the age of downsizing," *Sarasota Herald-Tribune*, 12 Jan. 1996, p. D1.

[11] "Cover Story: Managing by Values, Is Levi Strauss' Approach Visionary—or Flaky?" *Business Week*, 1 Aug. 1994, p. 49.

[12] Gary Moore, "Miracle Man," *Jacksonville*, May 1996, pp. 24-27 and 71.

[13] Robert Howard, "Values Make the Company: An Interview with Robert Haas," *Harvard Business Review*, Sept.-Oct. 1990, p. 143.

[14] Jennifer Reingold, "Executive Pay," *Business Week*, 21 April 1997, pp. 58-66.

[15] Warren Bennis, "Point of View: Worker's high anxiety about jobs may lead to era of social unrest," *Florida Times-Union*, 28 Feb. 1996, p. A17.

[16] Marjorie Kelly, "For Americans, having a job often means not having a life," *Minneapolis Star Tribune*, 19 Aug. 1996, p. D3.

[17] John A. Byrne, "How High Can CEO Pay Go?" *Business Week*, 22 Apr. 1996, pp. 100-06; and Jennifer Reingold, "Executive Pay," *Business Week*, 21 April 1997, p. 59.

[18] John A. Byrne, "Gross Compensation," *Business Week*, 18 Mar. 1996, pp. 32-33.

[19] Ibid, p. 34.

[20] Kenneth Labich, "Hot Company, Warm Culture," *Fortune*, 27 Feb. 1989, p. 74.

[21] Keith H. Hammonds, Wendy Zeller, and Richard Melcher, "Economic Anxiety," *Business Week*, 11 Mar. 1996, p. 61.

[22] "Who Are the Real Wealth Creators," *Fortune*, 6 Dec. 1996, p. 107.

[23] Kenneth Labich, "Making Diversity Pay," *Fortune*, 9 Sept. 1996, p. 180.

[24] Marjorie Kelly, "For Americans, having a job often means not having a life," *Minneapolis Star Tribune*, 19 Aug. 1996, p. D3.

[25] Keith H. Hammonds, "Balancing Work and Family," *Business Week*, 16 Sept. 1996, pp. 74-80.

[26] Sam Walton with John Huey, *Made in America* (Doubleday, 1992), pp. 144-45.

[27] Frank Rose, "A New Age for Business?" *Fortune*, 8 Oct. 1990, p. 164.

[28] Kahlil Gibran, *The Prophet* (Alfred A. Knopf, 1979), p. 56.

INDEX

About the Authors

John Zimmerman was the senior vice president and a director of Kepner-Tregoe, Inc., a world-renowned management consulting firm. **Benjamin Tregoe**, now serving as the company's chairman emeritus, was CEO and cofounder of Kepner-Tregoe. They are the coauthors of *Top Management Strategy* and *Vision in Action* (with Ronald Smith and Peter Tobia). Tregoe is also the coauthor (with Charles Kepner) of the seminal management books *The Rational Manager* and *The New Rational Manager*.